Meditations FOR A Powerful You

Meditations FOR A Powerful You

Simple life-changing practices to help you relax, recharge, and reconnect

Clare Connolly

CICO BOOKS
LONDON NEW YORK

To all the students of yoga and meditation who have been bothered enough to listen to me and kind enough to show up to my classes and practice with me in the past, present, and future. You are my inspiration, you are my joy!

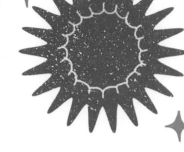

Published in 2024 by CICO Books
An imprint of Ryland Peters & Small Ltd

20–21 Jockey's Fields   341 E 116th St
London WC1R 4BW   New York, NY 10029

www.rylandpeters.com

10 9 8 7 6 5 4 3 2 1

A CIP catalog record for this book is available from the Library of Congress and the British Library.

ISBN: 978 1 80065 304 7

Printed in China

The information in this book is not intended to replace diagnosis of illness or ailments, or healing or medicine. Always consult your doctor or other health professional in the case of illness.

Illustrator: Gina Rosas Moncada
Commissioning editor: Kristine Pidkameny
Editor: Jenny Dye
Senior designer: Emily Breen
Art director: Sally Powell
Creative director: Leslie Harrington
Production manager: Gordana Simakovic
Publishing manager: Carmel Edmonds

Contents

Introduction/Intention

Can you feel your energy right now? This might be a difficult question. Have you ever felt tired, stressed, or even depressed? Have you ever felt joyful, in love, or deeply appreciative? Have you ever observed how your energy changes when you experience these different emotions? Generally, when you're sad or in grief or despair you'll feel tired and heavy, and you might say your energy is quite low. In contrast, when you're excited, grateful, or in love your energy tends to feel upbeat and high. If you've felt any kind of emotion, and we all have as part of the human experience, then you have felt energy.

Throughout my entire life I have been intrigued by energy, how energy feels within my body, and practices that I can do to raise and uplift it.

Everything is energy and energy is all there is.

Life is supposed to be fun, joyful, and expansive. But we all seem to take it very seriously indeed. My intention is to provide you with an easy process that will help you to raise your energy and empower you to live a happier life, by bringing attention to different aspects of your life and using the simple tool of guided meditation.

You don't have to be a professional "meditator" to join me on this journey through meditation. In fact, you don't yet need to be able to meditate at all. All you need is the will to want to feel better and a curiosity about how you can. This book is designed for anyone, any age, whoever you are or wherever you live. You don't have to be a monk, hippie, or yogi, and you don't have to live in a cave or wear spiritual beads and robes to experience the effects of this book. Every single one of you—even you, suited and booted in the office, or you, out there grafting on the building site, or you, at home working hard

This book is for anyone and everyone because the same energetic life force runs within each and every one of us.

with the children—can benefit from the tools on the following pages.

My inspiration to teach originally came from my exploration of the ancient Eastern philosophies of Yoga, Taoism, and Buddhism. But I've also been profoundly influenced by many of the great teachers of our time (see page 139). The book is a culmination of what I've learned over the years, including teachings that have encouraged me to connect more deeply with myself, to take guidance from my own energy, and to empower myself into the human being (and indeed spiritual being) that I am today.

The meditations in this book, which are each supported by a recorded audio version (see page 140), have been designed to remind you, the reader, of your inner energy and power. Notice I said "remind you." This is something that, deep down, you already know. The meditations will encourage you

to take responsibility for your feelings, especially if or when uncomfortable situations arise. I offer meditations that will help you to rebuild your energy, get back your confidence, and relax and let go of unwanted feelings and emotions. They will also help you to reduce anxiety, manage stress, become more resilient, balanced, and focused, find deeper clarity, and also to reconnect with your heart, yourself, your goals, your desires, and your innate power and joy.

It is time for you to discover how powerful you really are!

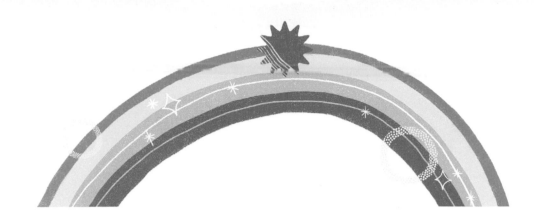

PART ONE

Getting Started

In this section you will explore the world of meditation. I begin
by answering frequently asked questions and addressing
limitations that many people have prior to starting a meditation
practice. Then we will dive deep into the fundamentals and
components of a meditation practice. Even if you are not
a beginner, you will enjoy Part One as it serves as a reminder
of not only how to meditate but also why we meditate. The final
pages of Part One are especially important as they tell you how
to use this book and provide information about the supporting
audio material and where you can find it.

Welcome: Who, What, When, and How?

On the following pages I will answer a few very common questions that I often hear about beginning and sustaining a meditation practice. It's natural to have many questions and perhaps even skepticism when starting, such as "can this really work for me?" or "I can't stop my thoughts and quieten my mind." So I simply encourage you to start with the feeling of curiosity, as though you are on an inner voyage of discovery.

I've heard the phrase "inner astronaut" before and I like this idea that you are literally exploring the space within yourself. Begin your meditation practice as if you were a child learning something brand new for the first time; children have so much fun and are in awe of the littlest things. If you like, make a decision that you want to feel a bit better every day, and set an intention to bring light to this and discover how. A daily meditation practice has completely changed my life in so many ways, and my hope is that it will do the same for you, too.

Who Can Meditate?

ANYONE! There is a common misconception that meditating is just for monks or religious people. And yes, while it has its place in many religious practices, meditation can have a profound effect on anyone—that even means you. You'll learn more about how meditation can improve your body, brain, heart, and energy in the chapters to follow.

What Is Meditation?

Meditation has been practiced for thousands of years and its power is still felt now by millions of people all around the world. The word "meditation" that we use today comes from the Latin word *meditatum*, which means "to concentrate" or "to ponder."

There are many other ancient translations of the word "meditation" that capture its essence, for example:

- Contemplation

- Mental development

- Mental training

- Becoming familiar with the mind

- Inner vision

- Observations

- Looking within

I love these translations. They are all helpful in truly understanding what meditation has always been and what it still is today, and why it could be useful for us too.

Meditation is something to practice so we can:

- Discover more about ourselves

- Find some peace and settle the mind in a fast-moving world

- Improve focus and concentration

- Manage stress better

- Have the time to visualize our dreams and desires

- Break bad habits and create more health, abundance, and love in our lives

- Connect to what is truly important and improve our mental health so we are able to feel just a little bit better every single day

When Should I Meditate?

That is completely up to you. And everyone is different. For many, a morning practice can be very powerful. When we sleep our brain activity slows down and we are not worrying, analyzing, or ruminating. When we wake up our brain activity speeds up and then we often start to think about our problems again. A morning meditation practice helps you to catch yourself right at the beginning of the day, while the brain is still remembering that dreamy, calm sleep state and before it has started to "worry" too much. Morning meditation will get you in a good-feeling place and ensure you get out "on the right side of bed," so to speak. It can set the entire tone for the day and be very nurturing. If you want to start a morning meditation practice, you can choose any meditation in the book that resonates with your mood on each given day, or simply start with the Morning Ritual meditation (see page 44).

Meditation can also be extremely helpful if you require a boost at any point throughout the day, perhaps to counter the mid-afternoon slump. You may also find meditation beneficial if you've had something or someone disturb your good vibes and you need to clear that heavy negative energy so you can feel lighter again. I find meditation very helpful if I am unwell and I need to stimulate my immune system; it works miracles for me and I always feel better—you could say meditation can be a bit like medication! If you need a midday meditation to reset, pick from any of the ones in this book, depending on your mood and how you would like to feel. Be Here Now (see page 40) and Electric Mode (see page 132) are good options to recharge your energy.

If you struggle with sleep, you may enjoy meditation to help settle the mind and allow you to drift off. We've all heard the phrase "never go to sleep on an argument"—if we do, we might find we wake up feeling just as angry at that person as when we went to sleep! During sleep we release all resistance and chatter in the mind, but as soon as we wake up, anything unresolved seems to arise almost immediately. If you go to sleep feeling annoyed or frustrated about something, you'll likely wake up feeling the same. Meditation at night helps you to release the day and dissolve any negativity and unwanted events, feelings, or emotions. It also helps you to feel good about the day whatever has happened, setting a calm and peaceful tone for your sleep. This gives you a much better chance of waking up feeling energized, refreshed, and satisfied. Check out the Sleep Ritual meditation (see page 54) or any of the other meditations you are drawn to in this book, to help you get a blissful night's sleep.

How Do I Meditate?

When embarking on a committed meditation practice, it's important to realize that it won't always be perfect. I like to go by the idea that it is what it is on any given day. You can go months at a time where you feel like you're not getting anywhere, and then all of a sudden have a huge breakthrough—perhaps a mystical moment within your meditation that brings you a message or a deep feeling of connection, peace, and wholeness.

It is called a "practice" because we are constantly "practicing."

Meditation is traditionally practiced seated (mainly so you don't fall asleep!) and sometimes also lying down (if the aim is to fall asleep!). But you can also get yourself into a meditative state when you are walking or running in nature, and perhaps even swimming, driving, or dancing. Meditation is achieved when your mind is free from external intrusive input from your environment (the people, places, and things in your life), and you're able to switch off and focus deeply upon the landscape within.

Start by meditating for just five minutes and then work up to ten minutes and build your practice up to however long you feel that you need in order to shift your energy into a good-feeling place. When I sit to meditate (often for about 30 minutes to 1 hour), I make a commitment to myself to stay meditating until I sense my energy rise and I feel ready to continue my day.

Meditation is cumulative, so see if you can make it a part of your daily routine. Try to do it at the same time each day, and don't give up. If one day you have a bad meditation, don't let that put you off. It can be slow progress to begin with, but you will soon feel incredible and reap the benefits. Remember that it takes time for this to become a habit. I'd say, once you commit to it, give yourself three months to really give it a good go. Sometimes you'll feel too tired, but don't let that put you off. Your meditation will rejuvenate you. Use the time you've set aside to wake up through your meditation—it will be worth it, I promise!

Make a commitment to meditate until you feel your energy rise.

Many people think that to meditate you need to be able to completely empty your mind, but that is simply not the case. Think of your meditation as a moment of inner exploration. It's a time to take a look inside at what's really going on and breathe with that emotion, whatever it is, and simply be present with it. The idea of sitting with your emotions may feel daunting and you may find that you have a lot of fear around the idea of doing it—and that's normal. For the first couple of months of practicing regular daily meditation, I spent most of the meditation just thinking "I'm doing this wrong!" when actually that's a big part of the process. I had to ride that wave and you may too... remember this, though: you're not alone.

As I progressed and got more days and notches on my meditation belt, I realized that this "doubt" was all part of my journey. Suddenly I'd have fleeting moments of pure stillness, deep connection, and feelings of love and appreciation. Those moments may only last for one or two seconds to begin with, but for me they were blissful and I wanted more.

Now in my meditation practice (on a good day) I can get my body into a blissful state much more quickly. This feeling stays with me throughout my day and if I need a top-up, I just go to my comfy chair or to my bed and have another 5, 10, 20 minutes, or however long I need. I also practice HeartMath™ techniques and breathe into my heart—more about this on pages 24 and 78. I can truly say that a daily practice has changed my entire life. I feel grounded, solid, secure, and much more focused. I encourage you in your meditation to take a look at negative thought patterns and any tension or spaces within your body that don't feel so good, and with the power of your meditating mind, begin turning them into positive learning experiences. Uplift yourself gradually, using the power of your focused thought and the practice of gratitude. Life is not linear; we will still have good days and bad days, we will still have problems to solve and opportunities to navigate. But through the simple technique of meditation you can flow with more ease and see more beauty in the little everyday moments.

In this busy world meditation is a practice that allows us space. The space to think, the space to feel, the space to process, and the space to change.

It's time to transform your life!

Meditation Essentials: Your Powerful Breath, Body, Brain, and Heart

There are many different styles of meditation, both ancient and modern. I will guide you through techniques of mindfulness, contemplation, manifestation, silence, and methods backed by science. Before we get started, I want to make you aware of a few essential elements that will ensure you have the most success in your practice. These elements are your breath, your body, your brain, and your heart. They all play a vital role in your meditation.

Your Powerful BREATH

You are powered by your breath. It is the essence of all life on our planet. From the moment you took your first breath right through to the moment when you'll take your last, breathing is essential to being "alive," and you do it between 22,000–25,000 times a day, usually without thinking about it.

Breath speaks its own language which can be observed by its rhythms. It depends upon your emotional state and awareness in any given moment. When you are relaxed or even sleeping the breath is slow, long, and deep. When you are alert, stressed, or anxious the breath changes its rhythm dramatically, and

can become short and sharp. Sometimes you may even catch yourself holding your breath. Due to breathing being mostly an unconscious process that is intimately linked to your emotions and feelings, the variation of your breath, even down to its subtle nuances, can therefore be a direct key to greater happiness, health, and wellbeing.

Breathing or respiration is a process of the autonomic nervous system, which deals with the processes in your body that you don't think about, such as digestion and blood pressure. Because the breath is automatic, this is why it alters in pattern and tempo depending on where we are, who we are with, and what we are doing. When we are in "fight, flight" mode (that feeling you need to either fight or run), the stress hormone cortisol is triggered and we enter what we know as the sympathetic nervous system. The breath rate increases to allow more oxygen to go to the brain so you can make faster decisions related to your survival. It is important that the body responds in this way; however, we can't live in a stress and survival state all the time as that would be exhausting. When we slow down the breath, we allow the body and the mind to rest, restore, and repair and this is the moment the stress hormone leaves the body and gets replaced by DHEA (often referred to as the body's natural anti-depressant), which can soothe neurotransmitters in the body. We then move into the parasympathetic nervous system. The body relaxes and the energy channels open up, allowing oxygen and energy to reset the body back to greater health, bringing us to a state known as homeostasis.

For over five thousand years the ancient yogis and sages in northern India have been controlling their breath through meditative processes such as yoga and breathwork exercises called pranayama, which you'll find examples of in this book. In yoga it is believed that a person's breath carries their subtle (I like to call it magical) energy or life force, which is often referred to by yogis (people who practice yoga) as "prana." The yogis believe that breathwork practices help us to clear out emotional and physical resistance or tension within the body so that greater energy and prana are free to flow.

In times when you're feeling unsteady, uneasy, or unsure, breathing mindfully can feel very grounding—try this through the Be Here Now (see page 40) and Mindful Moment (see page 38) meditations. Breathing mindfully can also feel energizing and exhilarating, which you can have fun with in Breathing Heart (see

page 76) and Electric Mode (see page 132). Breathing through a meditative practice has a multitude of other benefits such as stronger lungs and increased lung capacity, deep states of calm and peace, and increased focus and clarity in the brain. It may also help to reduce inflammation and improve cardiovascular health.

So take this opportunity to take a deeply nourishing inhale... a soothing, relaxing exhale... and let's continue.

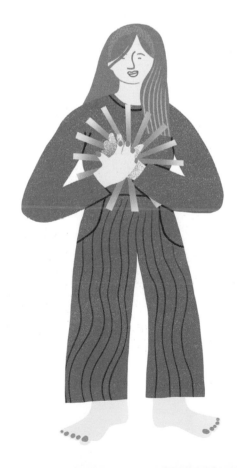

Your Powerful BODY

Take a moment to think about your body... really think about it... okay, was that difficult? What did you think? Did you think mostly about how it looks, and about its size, shape, and weight? The color of your skin perhaps? Your self-confidence or self-worth? Did you think about the pain you're experiencing? Or perhaps the limitations depending on your age and physical abilities?

THE ENERGY CENTERS

SEVENTH ENERGY CENTER
Colors: Violet/Bright white; **Location:** Crown of head and 12 inches (30 centimeters) above
Associations: Wholeness, Universal Energy, higher powers
Related to: The energy of the entire Universe

SIXTH ENERGY CENTER
Color: Indigo/Purple; **Location:** Third eye, brain
Associations: Intuition, mysticism, creativity
Related to: Pituitary and pineal glands

FIFTH ENERGY CENTER
Color: Blue; **Location:** Throat
Associations: Truth, freedom, empowerment
Related to: Thyroid glands

FOURTH ENERGY CENTER
Color: Green; **Location:** Heart center
Associations: Love, compassion, respect
Related to: Thymus glands

THIRD ENERGY CENTER
Color: Yellow; **Location:** Solar plexus
Associations: Confidence, willpower, health
Related to: Adrenal gland

SECOND ENERGY CENTER
Color: Orange; **Location:** In front of sacrum
Associations: Safety, strength, security
Related to: Digestive glands

FIRST ENERGY CENTER
Color: Red; **Location:** Root or base of spine
Associations: Grounding, passion, life force
Related to: Reproductive glands

Whatever you think about your body, the truth is you are made up of much more than just flesh and bone. You are elements such as oxygen, carbon, and hydrogen, and you are proteins, water, muscle, fats, connective tissues, hormones, systems, and processes. All of these are made up of cells and in every single cell there are trillions of atoms. In the center of the atom there is nothing, only energy waves. Since you are a collection of atoms that means you are pure energy—that is miraculous!

The ancient yogis believed that we have over 72,000 energy channels within the body in which the energy moves. Many of these are so small they cannot even be seen through a microscope. Through these channels (which are said to look like tiny fine glass tubes), the energy or *prana* flows. But these energy channels can become blocked or stagnant through tension, emotion, or injury.

The main central energy channel through which all energy flows in the body, and the one we will focus on the most, runs along the spine and is called the *sushumna*. This is where the energy centers, often referred to as Chakras, are located (see image opposite). The energy centers are not a myth, they are points in the body that contain concentrated amounts of energy, and they correspond to where glands are located. Glands secrete hormones. Hormones are chemicals that instruct processes in the body such as growth, blood pressure, glucose levels, temperature regulation, fertility, sex drive, metabolism, and sleep.

In Part 2, the meditation section of the book, you will find seven chapters. Each chapter pays close attention to a specific energy center within the body and the emotional signature of that center (see also the diagram on page 18). Seven chapters, seven energy centers. Energy is said to rise through the energy centers, as it will within you too as you practice.

A moving meditation practice such as yoga, running, or dancing can easily help to shake up the energy, releasing parts of the body that feel tight and allowing the energy to flow more freely. See the Walking into Confidence (page 70) and Step into Your Future (page 100) meditations. However, even a static practice can help to free up tension and open up the energy channels. Just by focusing and using your attention, you can learn to balance the hormones within the body. Whatever your mind is focusing on is where your energy goes. When energy is flowing, you will feel it and it will empower you! Meditation can help reframe negative thoughts about the body, build resilience, and help us to connect more deeply with the body.

Since the body is a vehicle for your soul and where "you" live, it is an important part of your meditation practice.

Interoception and Proprioception

Interoception and Proprioception are two techniques we use within meditations. Interoception refers to the process of looking and feeling inward, for example connecting to your body, breath, and feelings. The process of proprioception refers to the relationship of your body and the space around you, and being able to expand your awareness into it. If you'd like to listen to the audio recordings for these two techniques, turn to page 140.

Let's Practice Interoception

Introception is the process of looking and feeling inward.

To try this process out, locate and bring your attention inside the various parts of your body listed below. Spend a little time on each, say five breaths, and bring your attention to that place and notice any feelings or emotions. Then move on to the next. Close your eyes as you focus on each body part.

Focus inside:

1. Your head...

2. Your eyes...

3. Your nose...

4. Your ears...

5. Your mouth... even inside your mouth.

6. Your brain. See if you can feel it existing within your body, the left hemisphere and the right hemisphere.

7. Your heart.

8. Continue to try this all around your body. Arms, legs, torso, and various organs if you are able to locate them.

We will use this technique a lot in the meditations in this book.

Let's Practice Proprioception

Proprioception is the process of sensing where you are located within the space of your external environment.

To try this process out, close your eyes and see if you can sense the following. Take five slow breaths as you try to sense each one.

1. How far away the wall or an object is from your right shoulder...

2. How far away the wall or an object is from your left shoulder...

3. The crown of the head to the ceiling or right up into the whole of space above you to infinity.

4. The weight of your body into the earth and sensing through the ground to the earth's core.

5. Try dissolving the physical body completely and merging it with the energy of the space around you. Notice what that feels like.

We will also use this technique a lot throughout this book.

Your Powerful BRAIN

The brain is the most intricate part of our human bodies. There is not a second of the day when it is not processing, interpreting, initiating, and controlling. But do you ever give it much thought? (Haha—no that is not a joke!) How often do you spend time actually doing things that are good for and helpful to your brain, and furthermore, acknowledging or even being aware that you are? Everything has momentum, which is defined in the *Oxford Dictionary* as "the ability to keep increasing or developing."

Have you noticed that whatever you think about seems to get greater and whatever you practice you get better at? The same goes for your thoughts. What thoughts are you thinking and what thoughts are you practicing? It might be fair to say that whatever you place your attention on and therefore your energy on, increases or gets bigger.

If you think negative thoughts and continue to think them, those neurological connections begin to wire stronger together in the brain. The same goes for thinking positive thoughts. Think positive thoughts more often and those connections get wired stronger together. If we keep up our positive mental attitude, the old unused connections will eventually dissolve away. But we have to be dedicated and committed to want that change.

You get to decide and that decision starts with you and the choices you make inside your brain.

You have the choice...

Would you rather live a miserable, complaining, dull, negative life?

Or would you rather live an exciting, joyful, abundant, loving, positive life?

Through meditation, and as the Tibetans describe it, "becoming familiar with," we can begin to understand our unwanted thoughts, patterns, and behaviors. From this place of recognizing what they are, and naming them even, we can begin to lovingly reframe them and create new connections to quite literally change our minds, and subsequently our lives.

Our thoughts create our beliefs, and what we believe we become.

A major battle many people come across in meditation is settling the mind, and this might be the main barrier you face when beginning your meditation practice. The yogis recognize this busy, cluttered, restless, and sometimes chaotic mind, and they call it the "Chitta Vritti" or "Monkey Mind." The monkey is playful and wants to trick you. It keeps finding things to focus on that are unhelpful. Your job is to stay consistent in training your mind and lovingly, without judgment, reminding it to relax and come back to its natural state of balance.

I look at training my mind in the same way you would help a small child to learn or train a dog—with positive reinforcement. If my puppy, Hicks, does something wrong, I don't shout at him and berate him for his actions, he doesn't know better, I lovingly correct him with compassion and remind him of the correct way to behave. And then continue to repeat and practice until he understands. What I'm saying is, don't get angry or frustrated with yourself when you feel like you're not getting it or if you're having a particularly negative day. Be compassionate, know this is all part of the process and that you're living the human experience. No emotions are wrong—feel them, accept them, and lovingly soothe yourself back onto the path that feels better (see page 38).

As you'll learn in the Sleep Ritual meditation (see page 54), sleep is vital for focus, concentration, energy, your immune system, harmonious relationships, and much more. Imagine being able to get all the benefits of sleep also through your meditation practice.

This is meditation's power!

Your Powerful HEART

Your heart never gets a day off. It works endlessly 24 hours a day, 7 days a week. The main roles of your heart are to pump oxygen around your body, circulate nutrients and hormones to the correct places, and carry waste gases such as carbon dioxide back to the lungs so they can be removed from the body via your exhalation. The heart has a dynamic rhythm and produces a larger source of electromagnetic energy than anywhere else in your entire body, which you feel every time the heart beats!

In 1991, Dr. Drew Armour discovered that the heart is in effect a mini brain. It contains around 40,000 of its own brain cells (neurons) and has the ability to feel.

Simultaneously, Doc Childre and the HeartMath® Institute in the United States began researching the heart and they have, and continue to, help us understand the science of the heart on a deeper emotional level.

Have you felt your heart feel?

Most of us have experienced some form of heartbreak in life such as the loss of a loved one or a relationship. It's tough—you actually feel the heart ache and it can be deeply painful. But it's not only heartbreak that the heart feels. The heart feels everything from "energy-depleting emotions" such as depression, guilt, blame, sadness, and unworthiness, to "energy-renewing emotions" including joy, excitement, abundance, wholeness, love, and freedom. By bringing our attention to the heart in meditation, through using HeartMath® tools and simply breathing, we can open the heart back up to more positive, uplifting states that can feel deeply nourishing and help us to heal. We will look much deeper into how we can open our hearts in Chapter Four of Part Two, Connection (see page 74).

My Experience with HeartMath®

I have had the pleasure of working with HeartMath since 2023 and witnessing the benefits of their techniques first hand in my own practice and with other practitioners and students of HeartMath.

Due to the way that the heart and the brain are in constant communication, HeartMath found that more information travels from the heart to the brain than the other way around. They found that your emotions can affect the rate that the heart beats, and the rate the heart beats can in turn affect your emotions. You can read hundreds of incredible papers into the science of the heart at www.heartmath.org.

Off the back of all their research, HeartMath developed many techniques (see the Inner-Balance™ Technique on page 79) to help bring the heart and the entire nervous system into balance, harmony, and what they call "Coherence."

Try a HeartMath® technique now called Heart Focused Breathing™ which is explained in the box below, to allow you to connect to your heart's intelligence. You can have your eyes open or closed.

The meditation practices in this book will reconnect you back to your breath, your body, your brain, your heart, your feelings, and your emotions, dreams, and desires.

You will cultivate more peace, calm, joy, and appreciation, which in turn creates a deep sense of wellbeing, greater health, and even the ability to heal.

Heart Focused Breathing™ from HeartMath®

(For audio version see page 140)

Focus your attention on your heart. Imagine your breath flowing in and out of your heart or chest area, and breathe a little slower and deeper than usual.

Suggestion: Inhale for five seconds and exhale for five seconds, or whatever is comfortable.

How to Use This Book

Unless you're living in an ashram you're unlikely to have your own personal meditation teacher on hand 24/7 to help you learn, but a book can be picked up at any time. The meditations in the following chapters can be followed consecutively if you wish, slowly allowing your energy to rise each day with the next meditation in the book. Or you can flick through the pages, just as you would a recipe book and choose a meditation that corresponds to how you're feeling on any given day. You may be tired and need more energy, you may be wanting to start a morning or evening meditation practice, you may be suffering a grief or a misalignment within a relationship. There are a variety of meditations to choose from.

I encourage you to have an open mind and to practice the meditations you enjoy over and over. You might choose to practice the same meditation for a week or a month until you feel like you have truly mastered it before moving on. There is no right or wrong way to use this book. Do whatever feels right to you. Perhaps leave the ones that don't resonate with you right now and who knows, in 2–5 years or even in 10 years, they might be just what you are looking for.

If you enjoy these meditations, share the book with friends. You could get a meditation group together. Meditating in groups can be extremely powerful, as you all drift off on your own beautiful energetic journey and work together to feel uplifted.

If you want to be fully immersed, perhaps consider going on a yoga or meditation retreat. It always helps to meet like-minded people you can share your experiences with.

Audio Content

Using a book to learn to meditate used to be difficult because it can be hard to follow the instructions with your eyes closed. Now with the wonders of the internet and apps we have also created corresponding audio content to go alongside each meditation.

I advise you to read through the meditation in the book first so that you know what you are doing—after all, knowledge is power. Knowing what you are doing and why really helps the brain to achieve success in your meditations.

If you'd like to listen to the recorded meditation audio to guide your meditation, see page 140 for instructions on how to use the QR codes, or go to www.powerfulyoubook.com and choose the corresponding meditation audio link. I recommend that you listen through headphones, if you have them, for a more immersive experience.

Setting an Intention

At the start of your meditation practice it is always good to set an intention. An intention can be a word, a short sentence, or a mantra that reminds you why you are meditating. I offer some guidance about this before each meditation, but you're always welcome to choose your own intention, too.

Intention Set as

... a word

This is usually something you want to feel. It could be a word that uplifts you, for example, or one that makes you feel energized, expansive, joyful, at ease, calm, or peaceful, to name a few (I'm sure there are many other feelings and emotions you can think of, too).

... a sentence

You can put your word into a short sentence. It could be something like, "I intend to raise my energy," or "I feel the energy of calm and peace," or "I offer my practice today to the benefit of others." Allow yourself to be creative with your intention so that it is deeply personal to you and your desires.

... a mantra

Mantra in Sanskrit means "tool of the mind," and it can be a sound such as "Aum" or "Ohhhhm," or it can be something from an ancient text that you chant. Mantras are tools that help you to focus and bring you into higher states of consciousness.

Closing a Meditation

Once you finish your meditation it's always beneficial to close by bringing your palms together in a prayer gesture at the heart center, just in front of the chest, and offer thanks either to yourself or to a higher being such as God or a guardian angel.

A yogi term to end with is Namaste, which means, "the divine in me recognizes the divine in you/others." It's also good to remind yourself to "be receptive," and open up to life as you continue with your day or week.

It's time to meditate...

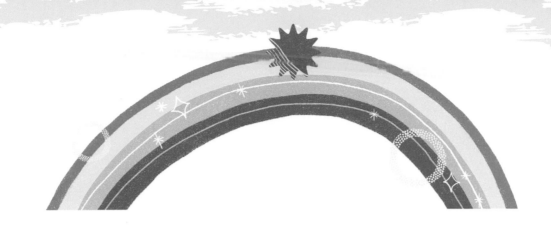

PART TWO

Meditations

Here you will find 28 meditations that will help you to reconnect with your body and mind, find balance in your life, build confidence, open your heart, discover your truth, create the future you desire, and help you to live a more energized, grateful, and expansive life! I practice all these meditations myself and they have also helped guide many of the yoga students I have taught over the years. Each one has a short intro so you can understand exactly what you're hoping to achieve. I wish you luck, love, and bright vibes as you embark on this journey into meditation and encourage you to be receptive.

Chapter One

Presence

Being fully present is powerful.

From a grounded, present place where you are self-aware, you allow yourself the space to assimilate and interpret what's in front of you or within you. You're able to be focused and engaged. You're able to appreciate the little things. You allow yourself the time to respond to others with care and kindness and you are able to be more intentional with your time and your response to life as it is happening. The simple act of being present can help to decrease stress, anxiety, and depression and help us to live in every moment with greater ease and purpose.

Everything is temporary.

Living in the present is also a useful time to acknowledge that everything is temporary. This is especially helpful to remember when you're going through a difficult patch in your life. Remember that every second of your life is completely unique and every new second is a chance to stop and then begin to create something new—there will be no time exactly the same as this right now ever again.

The meditations in this section will help you to feel grounded, sure, and focused in the NOW and engage in gratitude for all we have in this moment. Living in the present engages all your senses, your body, mind, and heart, and surrenders them to the powerful present moment, cultivating a steady peace and bliss.

Meditations in this chapter

Arriving: *Meditation for new beginnings*

Welcome to the first meditation, which is quite appropriately called Arriving—you have now truly arrived in this book. As we go through our lives, we constantly encounter new situations, and each one brings about a shift in energy. Whether it's stepping into a new environment or meeting new people, each arrival is an opportunity to ground ourselves in the present moment and connect with our surroundings.

Have you ever felt that your body has arrived somewhere new, but your soul is not quite there yet? I felt this recently when I moved house. It took my soul a little time to catch up with all the changes of not only a new bed to sleep in, but a new journey to work, new faces on the streets, and new roads and paths to navigate and explore. For a while I felt like I was "all over the place."

In this meditation we begin by activating the first energy center, which is located just in front of the base of the spine. It governs our reproductive organs and contains enough energy to literally create life. Activating this center will help us to feel grounded and connected. Then we will acknowledge a practice from the Buddhist philosophy called "Gladdening the Mind," which never fails to uplift my energy and make me smile. In this meditation, we will focus on cultivating a sense of mindfulness and awareness as we "arrive," allowing us to fully embrace the experience and the energy that comes with it.

INTENTION
Today I intend to fully arrive with power, strength, and a smile.

A note for practicing Lion's Breath
In this meditation you will practice Lion's Breath. Take a large breath in through the nose and then exhale powerfully, sticking the tongue right out of the mouth all the way to the chin, make the sound of a lion's roar, and feel your entire face stretch! If this feels too silly or if you feel too self-conscious, then just breathe deeply instead.

MEDITATION (FOR AUDIO VERSION SEE PAGE 140)

1. Begin in a seated position and start by taking three Lion's Breaths to cleanse and release out any frustration, anger, stress, and tension in the face. Allow this breath to wake you up and bring you to right where you need to be and right where you are, right now.

2. Be comfortable, close your eyes, and allow your attention to focus between the eyebrows. Breathe into that space. Just be the observer of your thoughts, witnessing any fluctuations of the mind, and notice these without any judgment. Spend a few minutes here.

3. Now draw your attention to your body and focus your mind on the space just in front of the base of your spine. See the color red as a red wheel of energy spinning in this space. Breathe into this rich color. Allow this energy to ground you.

4. Now imagine a smile appearing inside the red light. The smile travels down through the whole of your pelvis, into your legs, feet, and toes and into the earth.

5. The smile travels to the organs and muscles within the abdomen. The red light is glowing and smiling.

6. The smile moves into the upper torso, up into the chest, the heart, and lungs.

7. Feel the smile moving down from your shoulders through your arms, into your hands, fingers, and thumbs. And moving upward into your neck, your skull, and all the features of your face.

8. Have an awareness that you are in this meditation right now. Feel grounded and alive with this warm red glow of smiling energy. Enjoy it and let it allow you to arrive today, however you wish. Cultivate feeling poised and strong, a sense of ease and purpose, freedom, and flow. Can you imagine what that feels like?

9. Contemplate other ways you could show up today and the feelings you wish to generate as you do. Then mindfully glide your way into the rest of your day.

Be receptive—Namaste.

FIRST ENERGY CENTER/RED WHEEL OF LIGHT ENERGY
Associations: Grounding, passion, life force

Cycle of Life: *Connecting in nature*

Everything has its seasons and cycles, not just the planet. Everything is a constant cycle, from each new task in each new hour, to each new day, and each new season and each new year. In our ever-expanding life and world there are always things that come up... life is transient and constantly changing and evolving, as are you.

We experience new life, we experience death, we make new friendships and relationships, things end, things start, and things transform and change.

Taking a moment in time to acknowledge this wonderful planet can feel deeply nourishing. The magnificent earth, our giant rock made of minerals and gases that spins on its own axis, is constantly turning from day to night and from night back to day. It is surrounded by our moon, planets, and stars in the vastness of our solar system in open space and to infinity and beyond. To think about space and the idea of infinity boggles my mind and makes me wonder what it is all about. I find joy in consciously marveling at these things because it all comes back to energy and that makes me feel powerful. How about you?

In this meditation we will reconnect to the cycles of nature and be present with accepting the change that it presents to us. In this practice, we will explore how we can cultivate a deeper sense of awareness and connection with the natural world around us, and how we can learn to embrace the ebb and flow of life with a sense of openness and acceptance.

Through this practice, you may find greater peace, joy, and meaning in your life. You can practice this meditation outside, fully immersed in nature and at different times of the year to really feel the power of the changing seasons. If for some reason you can't be outside, it is also fine to practice this in a comfy chair at home, with the vision of the natural world inside your mind.

INTENTION
I feel nature's life force replenishing and rejuvenating me.

MEDITATION (FOR AUDIO VERSION SEE PAGE 140)

1. Arrive in your meditation space, either out in your garden, in a local park, or in a forest. Somewhere you can feel safe and be uninterrupted. If the weather is bad outside and you're at home, let your imagination take you to whatever beautiful scene of the natural world that you wish to go to.

2. With your eyes open, look around and allow yourself to take in the landscape of your surroundings. Notice the different shades of colors. What can you see? Take in the pages of this book and whatever else is beyond it, in front of you, behind you, and all around you. Explore your environment or imagine the vista around you. Then gently close your eyes and take a moment to look deeply within at your inner landscape.

Notice... any thoughts in the mind.

Notice... any tension, tightness, or unease in the body.

3. If your body needs to move a little to release, take your arms out to the side or up over your head into a big stretch. Give your body what it needs right now... and once you've done that, bring yourself to stillness.

4. Now bring your attention to your breath. Picture a circle. Your slow inhalation is half the circle, and your slow exhalation completes the circle. Visualize this in whatever way feels right to you. You may imagine you are drawing the circle on a page, or you could imagine seeing it on a screen. This is the cycle of your breath. Inhale and Exhale. Always connected.

5. This is a sacred pause in nature. Be present right now. Take a little time to enjoy each of the next steps.

• Firstly feel the weight of your body into the ground. Let it surrender to gravity and feel the muscles relax a little deeper in the safe space you are in.

- What does the temperature feel like where you are? Move your hands around in the air, or feel the gentle breeze around your shoulders and neck.

- Can you smell anything in the air? The flowers, the earth, or vegetation?

- Now what can you hear—birdsong, planes, traffic, the wind, the sound of a gentle stream? Remember these sounds can be all within your imagination too.

- Can you taste anything in your mouth right now? Take a couple of breaths in through the mouth just to taste the air.

6. Close your eyes again and come back to your breath and your vision of the circle of your breath. Bring your breath back into equal lengths on the inhale and exhale.

7. Now allow your mind to drift off with one or more of your senses, enjoying whatever it is you choose and lingering upon it. Perhaps you're fascinated by a particular sound or feeling within your body—relax into it and surrender to it. Continue to breathe deep breaths and enjoy the feeling of connecting to this beautiful moment.

8. As you bring your attention back, imagine it is returning to a brand new reality, a fresh sense of energy. A change for you, a reset, and the start of a brand new cycle in your life. What does it feel like to be excited for change? Is it a chance to grow, evolve, or start again?

9. Slowly blink open your eyes and take in the natural world once again. Perhaps everything feels more vivid, as if in high definition as all your senses are heightened to this new moment. Spend a few minutes basking in the beauty. Feel nature's life force replenishing and rejuvenating you.

10. Notice whether you've had any little shifts in your energy and carry this feeling with you into your day, week, month, year, and beyond.

Be receptive—Namaste.

Mindful Moment: *Breathing, grounding, and living in the present*

Welcome to this meditation on the mindful present moment. We will begin with a powerful breathing technique called box breathing, to ground you in the present moment. Box breathing (see the instructions in the meditation opposite and the diagram below) has been used for many years in the military and special ops (particularly by the U.S. Navy Seals) as a secret tool to help calm stress and get focused.

We will then move into a body scan that will connect you deeply with the sensations and experiences of the now. Take a few deep breaths and allow yourself to fully embrace this moment of peace and mindfulness.

A body scan is a very simple technique to allow your whole mind, body, and your emotions to reset. It comes from a Yogic practice called Yoga Nidra, which means Yogic Sleep. Despite the name, the idea in this practice is that you stay awake and consciously relax. It is said that 20 minutes of Yoga Nidra is as good as 4 hours of actual sleep. So this is a great practice if you have a mid-afternoon slump and you just need to restore a bit of energy. It would be a good meditation to do before the next meditation (Boost Your Energy, see page 40), if you'd like to extend your meditation practice and do two meditations back to back, or it can just be practiced on its own.

INTENTION
I am gently guided back to stillness.

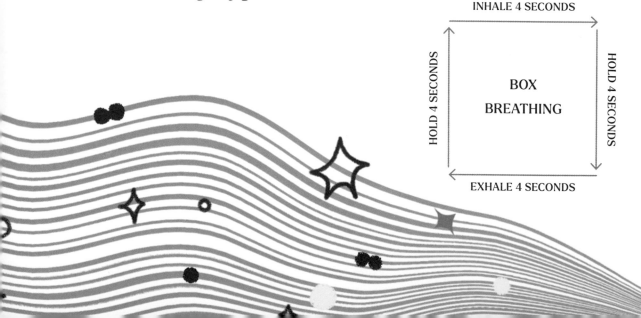

INHALE 4 SECONDS

HOLD 4 SECONDS

BOX BREATHING

HOLD 4 SECONDS

EXHALE 4 SECONDS

MEDITATION (FOR AUDIO VERSION SEE PAGE 140)

1. Find a place where you can be comfortable. Realize that you don't have to make any effort at all to notice the natural feeling of just being. Be here with your body and with your breath. Take a moment to be still.

2. Begin box breathing: Inhale through the nose for a count of 4 (count slowly in your head 1, 2, 3, 4), then hold for a count of 4, exhale through the nose for a count of 4, and hold for a count of 4, and hold again for 1, 2, 3, 4. Continue for roughly 8 complete rounds, all the time breathing through your nose. Observe how this breath makes you feel.

3. Now come to a natural relaxed breath and just breathe for the pleasure of breathing. Noticing any thoughts that come to mind. You could even imagine your breath like the ocean waves. As you're inhaling, the wave rises and builds energy, and when you're exhaling, it crashes and tumbles, releasing any tension.

4. Bring the whole of your awareness to your head. Relax the skull, ears, eyebrows, and eyeballs in their sockets. Relax your nose, your cheeks, your mouth, and jaw. Be aware of the space inside the head and the space around the head.

5. Next, bring your awareness to the neck. Swallow and relax the throat. Relax all the muscles and fibers of the shoulders. And relax right down both arms, to the hands, fingers, and thumbs. Be aware of the space within the arms and the space around the arms.

6. Relax the body deeply—the whole of the torso. Relax the heart, lungs, stomach, the entire digestive system, and the reproductive system. Feel the organs relax backward in the body, sinking toward the earth. Notice the space inside the body and the space around the body. Heavy head, heavy arms, heavy body.

7. Finally, relax the legs, then relax right down the legs into the feet and toes. Be aware of the space within the legs and the space around the legs. Feel the body sink and almost dissolve into the surface beneath you. Spend time here, bathing in this perfectly mindful present moment.

8. Focus your mind now between your thoughts, on that moment where one thought has ended and the next has not yet begun. If your mind wanders, gently guide it back to the silence—the space and emptiness between your thoughts. Enjoy it. Stay as long as you need, until you feel ready to slowly move yourself back into your day.

Be receptive—Namaste.

Be Here Now: *Boost your energy*

Sometimes we just need a boost! Feeling present, focused, and energized can be truly exhilarating. In this day and age there are so many things to distract us. Do you ever feel like you have a hundred and one things to do and not enough time? Time-shortage consciousness is real. You might have your social media, hobbies, fitness, work, emails, text messages, phone calls, meetings, people to see, things to do—there is so much to keep up with. We try to fit in vacations and meet-ups with friends, but we are all so busy.

There certainly isn't enough time to meditate! Or is there? The thing is...

> *I have found that when I make the time to meditate, everything else is easier.*

If I am super busy but I still fit in that meditation, everything else flows with greater ease and clarity. My words won't teach you this—you'll need to try it and experience it for yourself. Meditation clears a path for me for the rest of the day to get things done. I hope it does the same for you too.

This meditation aims to deeply ground you to the earth while opening up the main channel of energy, the *sushumna* (see page 19), right up the entire spine to the brain, allowing a free flow of energy to boost and recharge. You'll find that you can learn to refresh, renew, rebuild, and sustain your energy, and by bringing awareness to your body and breath, you can tap into a deep source of vitality and rejuvenation.

For this meditation be seated, either cross legged on the ground or if you are on a chair, have your feet firmly planted on the earth.

INTENTION
I feel a renewed sense of life force, expansion, and clarity.

MEDITATION (FOR AUDIO VERSION SEE PAGE 140)

1. Find a comfortable seated position. Feel your spine lengthen as much as you are able from the bottom of the spine right to the crown of the head. Feel your shoulders, elbows, and wrists relax, lightly resting your palms open in your lap.

2. Take deep breaths in and out through the nose, right into the lungs and even into the belly. Let the breath be expansive and energizing.

3. Imagine a pool of energy about 12 inches (30 centimeters) below ground. You could visualize a pool of watery light glowing with silvers and blues. See this as the source of all energy, a gift from the earth.

4. Begin to breathe this energy up through the soles of the feet and into the lower legs. See the bright watery light moving into your body, beyond your knees, upper legs, and into your hips. Take your time.

5. Feel the spine opening up into a tube, like a giant translucent straw. And begin to feel this light energy flow upward, through and beyond all the organs in the torso, the reproductive organs, digestive organs, cardiovascular organs, and respiratory organs. Feel the energy flooding down both the arms into the fingertips, rising up into the skull and filling the brain with this bright watery light. Feel the brain tingle!

6. Now visualize a pool of energy about 12 inches (30 centimeters) above the head. It is like a vortex of all the energy in the universe—the energy that created the stars, the planets, and you.

7. The earth energy continues to flow until it meets the universal energy above your head. Let that energy be playful; let it swirl and dance in a way that feels invigorating.

8. Let this energy shower out, creating a fountain of light around your body— a giant force field of energy. Visualize it going back down to the pool in the earth, all the way back up through the body to the pool above your head. It is a constant stream of light and energy.

9. Notice how this makes you feel and enjoy its power. Alive, energized, dynamic, alert, motivated, invigorated. Feel the effect on your body and mind.

10. Begin to expand your energy field in all directions. With every breath the field grows bigger and brighter, until it encapsulates the room, then your entire street, city, and country, and so on until the whole of planet earth is in your energy field. This step may take some getting used to—for now just go as big with your energy field as feels comfortable.

11. When you're ready, bring your awareness back to your body and feel a renewed sense of life force, expansion, and clarity.

Be receptive—Namaste.

Chapter Two

Balance

Nature likes things to feel balanced.

Balance is a state of equilibrium where all things exist in harmony and work together. In nature, balance means that different species and ecosystems coexist and support each other. Within our wonderful bodies, balance refers to a state of physical, mental, emotional, and spiritual wellbeing, where different systems and functions are working together optimally—this is often referred to as a state of homeostasis (see page 17).

As human beings we crave to be in harmony with all of life and with each other, but life can and often does throw us off. Business, commerce, media, war, illness, and other people can create chaotic, sticky patches, and drama in our lives which we will need to navigate.

It's handy to remember that your mind and body are always in constant communication with each other...

- You'll notice this when, for example, you smell some delicious food, and a signal is sent to your brain and then your body has a response. It might be that the stomach rumbles and/or the mouth salivates.

- You will also notice this when you hear a piece of beautiful music and are emotionally moved, either to joy or to sadness, or that piece of music may give you goose-bumps. This is evidence that the mind and body are in constant communication.

Our job is to remain balanced and comfortable even though factors outside of us—the people, places, and things—are often unsteady. This is where meditation comes into its power for me.

When we are in balance it may feel like a sense of calmness, stability, and ease.

Meditation can be a useful tool to help achieve balance as it promotes relaxation, reduces stress, and improves focus. In this section, you'll find four meditations to help you feel more balanced throughout the full 24 hours of your day. The Morning and Sleep Ritual meditations are excellent ways to move back into a state of balance at these pivotal times, as soon as you wake up, to help you prepare for your day and before you sleep, to help release your day.

In Fight, Flight to Freedom, we will work with alternate nostril breathing to deeply balance and reset your nervous system. In Finding Your Equilibrium, we will tune into the frequency of your second energy center, which governs survival and is our center of safety and security.

Meditations in this chapter

Morning Ritual: *Seize the day*

A morning meditation practice will put you in a good, solid, grounded place and will set the tone for your entire day. You'll feel invigorated and be more focused and prepared. You'll get more things done and ensure you are able to show up as the most authentic, genuine, strong, powerful version of you.

Mornings are a fantastic time to meditate. And for me my morning rituals and practices are an absolute non-negotiable in my daily routine. I always love to meditate first thing every day and I never miss it.

But what if you have an early flight and have to be at the airport at 5 or 6am?... Well, I will still ensure there is enough time set aside for at least 15 minutes of either silent or guided meditation before I leave home for the airport.

Why?... The reason I meditate first thing in the morning is simply because it puts me in a good-feeling place. I can deeply feel the effect that a meditation practice has on my brain, my body, my health, my day, and my overall life in comparison to when I didn't have a regular morning meditation practice. When I started to meditate in the mornings, everything in my life began to fall into place and my hope is it will do the same for you too.

You might find that in the morning you just want to keep hitting the snooze button. I can confess to loving a good snooze at the weekends. However, I've found that 15–20 minutes of meditation in the morning, and more if I have the luxury of extra time, has an infinitely greater impact on my overall day than the 20 minutes of more snooze time, which usually seems to fly by in what seems like just a few seconds. To take any worry out of whether or not you have enough time, I suggest that you set your alarm for 15–20 minutes earlier than usual and use that time to meditate.

When you practice morning meditation, always sit up so that you're alert. I sit up in bed, but if you worry that you may fall asleep, then sit on a chair or on the floor with your lower back supported. You may even want to set another meditation alarm so you know when you need to move into the next part of your day.

Finding your routine might be difficult at first, but if you are determined to start your day in a great way—feeling energized and aligned—and actually do the meditation, you will soon reap the rewards and, like me, understand the power of this practice and no doubt always want to continue.

On the the next page you'll find a morning meditation practice to lift your energy and spirits. To follow the meditation, read step 1, then close your eyes and do the step before moving on to step 2, and so on.

INTENTION
Carpe diem (seize the day).

MEDITATION (FOR AUDIO VERSION SEE PAGE 140)

1. Begin in a comfortable seated posture with your spine straight, your shoulders soft, your face relaxed, and the crown of your head ascending upward.

2. Gently opening and waking up the body, bring your palms together at heart level and interlock your fingers. Turn the palms away from the body and take a big stretch, with your arms either out in front of you or lifted high to the sky. As you stretch, take three big energizing breaths.

3. Slowly release the arms down and rest the hands on top of the knees, with your palms open. Feel the energy of that stretch right from the crown of your head, down the arms, and through to the tips of your fingers.

4. Allow the breath to come to an even, natural rhythm, breathing exclusively through your nose. How are you feeling today? Take as long as you need to acknowledge your feelings.

5. Bring your awareness to the space 2 inches (5 centimeters) beneath your naval to your second energy center. Imagine a glowing orange wheel of energy here, and feel the warmth, security, safety, and strength of its glow.

6. Begin to see a bright white light between your eyebrows and expand both that light and the orange light from your second center out into the space around you, so your entire body is surrounded by a golden energy field of light energy: The energy of the sun and a brand-new day!

**SECOND ENERGY CENTER/
ORANGE WHEEL OF LIGHT ENERGY**
Associations: Safety, strength, security

7. Continue to breathe in through the nose and out through the nose. Breathe into this NEW vibrant light energy and enjoy it. Acknowledge this new day silently to yourself—"Today is a brand new day," "This day is unique, there is no other like it," "Every moment is precious and every new second is an opportunity to start again and come into my power."

8. Think of three things you will do today. Imagine yourself in each situation (as if like a mental rehearsal process) with a gentle smile on your face, a warm glow in your belly, and a feeling of satisfaction. If the situations present resistance, breathe until you feel that resistance soften. Give yourself about 30 seconds to 1 minute for each event. How will you present yourself in each scenario, how will each moment feel?

9. Now remind yourself that today there will still be other people, there will be technology, there may be commuters, transport and traffic, there will be agendas, there will be decisions to make, there will be surprises—good ones and not so good ones—there will be conversations, and each moment of today will be completely unique.

10. Come back to your glowing bright energy field of golden light. When you feel challenged today by things you can't control, gently encourage yourself to find your light, to find your energy and your power. Look for ways to take care of your energy, observing if things feel off and steering yourself back to a more grounded place.

11. Ask yourself these questions:

- How would it feel to flow through today with a sense of ease, feeling grounded and sure?

- How would it feel to have the ability to think with clarity and express with precision?

- How would it feel to experience freedom today, to mindfully choose your thoughts, feelings, and actions?

- How would it feel to have a really good day?

12. Place one hand onto your beautiful heart and take a few deep breaths. Allow your eyes to open and take in the brightness of the world around you now and the fresh opportunity ahead of you.

Today is going to be a really good day!

Be receptive—Namaste.

Fight, Flight to Freedom: *Balancing your nervous system*

"Fight, flight" is a process you may have heard of. It refers to the activation of the sympathetic nervous system, which is one of the functions of the autonomic nervous system (see page 16). When fight, flight is activated the adrenal glands produce cortisol which floods our body. Cortisol is a hormone and it is extremely important. Cortisol increases our heart rate to respond to danger; it also gets us out of bed in the morning, so we do need it! However, we don't wish to pump our body with cortisol all the time, as too much cortisol can lead to chronic stress and anxiety. All forms of stress impact our hormonal, physical, mental, emotional, and spiritual health, and can eventually compromise the immune system and even cause disease.

In this meditation we will practice alternate nostril breathing, which stimulates our parasympathetic nervous system. When we are operating from the parasympathetic nervous system (see page 17), the body decreases the amount of energy available for cortisol production in the adrenal glands and begins to produce a hormone called dehydroepiandrosterone (DHEA). DHEA is beneficial for reproduction, reducing fat on the body, increasing muscle mass, and for slowing down or even reversing the ageing process(!). It also helps to boost our immune system.

Alternate nostril breathing can be tricky, so read or listen to the instructions very carefully.

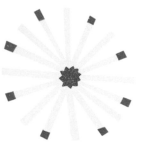

Vishnu Mudra

In this meditation you will need to also adopt a mudra or hand gesture. Using your right hand, bring the first two fingers (your index finger and middle finger) into the base of the right thumb. Lift your right hand to just in front of your face. You will use your right thumb to close off or block your right nostril. So just try that now, and release.

Then you will use the ring finger (the finger next to your little finger) to block off your left nostril—try that now and release. In this meditation, we will breathe alternately from one side to the other side. You will always use the right hand. If for some reason you need to use your left hand instead, however, that is fine too.

INTENTION

I am balancing the energy of my body and mind.

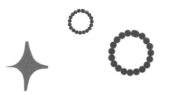

MEDITATION (FOR AUDIO VERSION SEE PAGE 140)

1. Sit up in a chair or cross legged, however you are most comfortable. Take a moment to notice your natural breath. Is it smooth or a little labored? Just observe.

2. Check in with how your mind is feeling today. Perhaps it is busy and chaotic; maybe you're feeling worried or anxious about something. Allow that emotion to just be—all emotions are allowed. It's good to recognize and acknowledge them and then work to release them so you can shift your energy.

3. Bring your right hand into Vishnu Mudra as explained on page 49. Take a full breath in through both nostrils and a full breath out through both nostrils.

4. Then bring your right thumb to close your right nostril, creating a seal. Breathe in through the left nostril slowly for a count of 6. At the top of the breath switch the nostrils, placing the ring finger of the same right hand on the left nostril, releasing the thumb on the right nostril, and exhaling through the right side for a count of 6. Stay here, keeping the left nostril blocked. Inhale through the right side for a count of 6, then at the top of the breath switch, so that the thumb now blocks off the right nostril. Exhale through the left for a count of 6... This completes one round.

5. Continue step 4 for about 8–12 more complete rounds. Once you get the hang of it, see whether you can do it with your eyes closed.

6. When you get to the final round, complete the alternate nostril breathing by exhaling through the left nostril. Relax both hands down now and rest them on your lap or knees, with your palms open.

7. Before moving back into your day, take a moment to just observe how you're feeling. Notice your breath, your body, your brain, and your heart. Calm, peaceful, and balanced.

Be receptive—Namaste.

Finding Your Equilibrium: *Reset back to where you feel strong*

In the *Oxford Learner's Dictionary*, equilibrium is defined as "a state of balance, especially between opposing forces or influences." We will meditate to tune in to and find that sweet spot in balance, our so-called inner compass, which guides us to where we feel steady and strong. In Buddhism this place is often referred to as "the middle way" or "middle path," and it is the place right between any extremes. It is where nothing is too excessive or impulsive, but it is also a place where we are not so carefree that we get nothing done and there is no structure to our lives. The Stoic interpretation is along the lines of "everything in moderation."

This is a powerful lesson and particularly important in this day and age, where there is so much addiction and attachment in people's lives. We use and attach to external things as a way of numbing our feelings, emotions, or pain. When I talk about addiction, I'm not only referring to drugs, alcohol, or sex, but also the addiction to our phones, click bait in the news, social media, shopping, television, negative self-talk and toxic relationships, to name but a few.

Imagine if we could reset the balance from the inside so that we didn't need to rely on anything outside ourselves to feel whole. What if we could let go of limiting emotions such as fear, rejection, guilt, blame, or obsessiveness and replace those feelings with a sense of safety, security, and creativity?

INTENTION
I am pure positive energy.

MEDITATION (FOR AUDIO VERSION SEE PAGE 140)

1. Start this meditation in a comfortable seated position. Imagine a piece of string lifting up through the whole of your spine, out of the top of your head, with your spine stretching upward toward it. Then relax your face. Let your shoulder blades slide down each side of the spine... and breathe. You can have the eyes closed or in a soft steady gaze downward.

2. As you breathe bring your palms to rest on your lower abdomen just underneath your belly button. Place the hands in a way that feels comfortable to you, either one on top of the other or side by side. Relax the elbows to the sides. Take the breath down deeply into the space behind your hands. As you inhale feel the hands rise, and as you exhale feel them fall. Feel every single breath calming and centering you.

3. Next, visualize a set of balancing scales and notice that the scales are off balance, so they are heavy on the left-hand side and light on the right-hand side. The left side represents your past and the right side represents your future. You are in your future... but way up in the air sitting or standing on the right side of the scales. As you continue to breathe here, begin to notice all the people, places, and things in your life that are weighing you down on the left side. See them all stacked up. These are things you apply great significance, over-importance, and a lot of seriousness to. They are things that you are attached to and they are weighing you down.

4. Choose one item on your scales that you feel you can release. See that thing either dissolve or lift up like a helium balloon, or perhaps it grows wings and flies away—however you would like to visualize it. Simply let it go. As each item disappears, feel the scale rebalancing a little.

5. Continue to focus on the things you are attached to and see if you can systematically let them go. Take your time with each; some will be easier than others. Focus.

6. You may not be able to rebalance the scales completely in one meditation—this might be a meditation that you return to over and over again for a few weeks or months.

7. When you feel as if you are as balanced as you can be today, guide your attention back to the space in the lower abdomen behind your hands. Imagine a warm orange glowing wheel of light warming into this space. Notice the freedom you feel from your release and enjoy this new lightness you have found. Breathe into this space, feeling a warm orange glow of safety, strength, and security.

8. Feel appreciation for your courage to let go and honor your ability to do this.

Be receptive—Namaste.

Sleep Ritual: *Preparing for a deep, blissful night's rest*

A good night's sleep is one of the best ways to renew our energy and can also improve overall physical and mental health, increase productivity and concentration, reduce stress and anxiety, and boost immune system function. We've all felt the effect of a lack of sleep and also unsettled sleep...

... So how can you ensure you get a restorative night's sleep every night? Train your brain!

Meditation can be used as a gateway to sleep, by helping to train your brain-wave patterns. During sleep the brain waves are slow, and we are no longer operating in the "analytical mind" where brain waves are much faster. Through meditation we begin to surrender our thoughts and allow our brain-wave patterns to slow down to a state that is more akin to the brain-wave patterns of when we are asleep.

The key to getting better sleep is to train your brain into these slower brain-wave patterns. After 20 years of yoga and meditation practice, I never ever have a problem getting to sleep—sometimes I can't even remember turning off the light! Every night I know exactly where my brain waves need to be for me to fall asleep and I can do it in a matter of seconds.

We all have what we call the monkey mind (see page 23), but part of meditating is learning how to calm the mind and train it; just in the same way an athlete trains their body for optimal performance. It's the same way you learn how to drive without thinking about it... you mirror, signal, maneuver and it feels automatic! Sleep is a function of the brain that you can also practice, and through practicing meditation you can get better at it.

Tips for getting a good night's sleep

Having good sleep habits or a routine in the evenings is also a helpful practice to adopt. This is often referred to as "sleep hygiene."

Here are some of my recommendations:

- Try not to look at your phone or laptop after 8pm, to give your mind a chance to start releasing "information" from the day.

- Take a nice warm bath or shower, brush your teeth, and make yourself comfortable and cozy in your pajamas.

- Take a few deep breaths before you get into bed and see if you can think of a couple of events in your day that you are grateful for. Try not to focus upon conversations and events from the day here, just keep your focus on things that went right and things that made you smile. This could be as simple as someone making you a cup of tea or a stranger smiling at you in the street. How does feeling grateful make you feel inside?

- Get excited about going to bed, and make it feel like an "event." Peel back the covers and feel the softness of the duvet on your hands and skin. As you climb into bed, begin to feel your muscles relax into the mattress and mindfully feel the pillow behind your head and neck. Notice the smell in the air. Perhaps add some drops of lavender oil to your pillow or use a pillow spray and breathe in the scent deeply.

- Set an intention to have a good sleep: "Tonight I will sleep deep, and relax and restore my body and mind." Intention setting is a great way to plan what is ahead of you and set the tone for your sleep.

- Then meditate. The Yoga Nidra (Yogic Sleep) on page 56 will guide you to relax through all your body parts and begin the sleep training. The main point here being that you allow yourself to let go.

You'll likely need to memorize this meditation or listen to the audio.

INTENTION
Tonight I will have a deep, relaxing sleep and wake up feeling refreshed and recharged.

MEDITATION (FOR AUDIO VERSION SEE PAGE 140)

1. Prepare your room for sleep using some of the suggestions on page 55 so that you can feel cozy and calm.

2. Now lay yourself down in your bed in the most comfortable position for you. I suggest lying on your back with your legs a little wider than your hips and your arms by your side, with your palms facing upward, or do whatever works for you.

Be steady and completely relaxed and still.

3. Prepare your mind for sleep by allowing yourself to finish off any conversations and release agendas and work. Take a brief moment to practice gratitude for the day you just experienced. Whether the day was easy or hard, be grateful for its lessons.

4. As you close your eyes, bring your attention to the heart and set the intention on page 55 quietly in your mind.

Relax. Relax. Relax.

5. Feel the weight and density of the body as it releases a little deeper into the mattress beneath you. Heavy arms, heavy legs, heavy torso, and heavy skull.

6. Take a deep breath in through the nose and sigh it out through the mouth. Repeat another couple of times if that feels good. You are now free to surrender... you are free to let go.

7. Bring your attention and awareness to your feet and relax the big toes, second toes, middle toes, fourth toes, and little toes. Relax all the tiny bones and muscles and joints of both the feet. Silently say to yourself, "I relax the feet, the feet are relaxed"... feel the feet dissolve into the space around you.

8. Bring your attention to your legs: the lower legs, knees, upper legs, and right up into the hips. Silently say to yourself, "I relax the legs, the legs are relaxed"... feel the legs dissolve.

9. Now bring your attention to the body. Relax the lower body, lower back, hip bones, pelvis, buttocks, and all organs of the lower body. Feel them melt deeper into your bed. Relax the belly and the mid-back and all organs of the mid-body. Relax the chest and the front of the rib cage, the back of the rib cage all around the ribs, and relax all the organs inside the rib cage. Relax the shoulders and shoulder blades. Feel them heavy into the bed. You are free to let them go. Silently say to yourself, "I relax the body, the body is relaxed"... feel the body dissolve.

10. Relax down both the arms, from the upper arms to the elbows, lower arms, wrists, and hands. Silently say to yourself, "I relax the arms, the arms are relaxed"... feel the arms dissolve.

11. Relax all the tiny bones and muscles of the hands, fingers, and thumbs, right through to the finger prints and thumb prints. Silently say to yourself, "I relax the hands, the hands are relaxed"... feel the hands dissolve.

12. Bring attention now to the throat. Swallow once, and relax the throat, the back of the neck, and the skull, imagining them heavy and sinking. Relax the ears, the cheeks, the jaw, the chin, the mouth, and inside the mouth... the teeth, tongue, and gums all relax. Relax the nose and the nostrils, up through the sinuses. Relax the eyeballs and let them roll back in the head. Relax the eyebrows, letting them slide away from one another. Relax the frown and let the brain relax in your skull. The body sinks down deeper into the mattress and the bed beneath you.

13. Leave your body by itself to rest and lift your mind up and away, into the darkness of space, floating through the stars in the twinkling night's sky. Send your awareness deep into the blackness of space.

Feel your body completely dissolve, as you drift off into a blissful night's sleep.

Good night.

Chapter Three

Confidence

Step back into your confident, authentic self—believe me there is no limit to just how good this can feel!

Confidence is an extremely powerful feeling that helps us to achieve our dreams and goals and empowers us to live up to our innate potential. Confidence, like every other emotion, is an energy. It's a feeling that can be practiced, nurtured, and strengthened, and on the other hand it can be depleted or even destroyed.

Over the past few odd years of lockdowns and uncertainty, many of my yoga students and coaching clients reported a drain on their confidence, or even losing their confidence completely in certain areas of their lives. Some lost confidence in their bodies as they had struggled with illness, others lost confidence in social situations and leaving the house after being cooped up for so long.

Since confidence is energy and all energy is a frequency, the good news is we can find it again. All we have to do is line up our own energy with the frequency of that feeling of being confident and then practice, practice, practice until it becomes neurologically wired and the thought, feeling, and emotion of confidence is second nature again.

A positive outlook, learning new things, and connecting with other people can all help you to lift, boost, and build confidence.

But there are also ways of connecting with yourself on a deeper level that allow you to harness your inner energy, alter your belief system, and feel better about yourself, lifting your spirits and inspiring greater confidence in your abilities. If I ask you, "How does it feel to be confident?", spend a moment thinking about the answer. To me it feels sure, joyful, clear-minded, strong, unlimited, free, and steady, just to name a few emotions—you may have thought of some other words. Remember them now and join me in this next chapter.

Meditations in this chapter

Locating Your Power:
Release anxiety and reclaim your identity 60

Your Confident Body:
Feeling great in the skin you're in and trusting your body 64

The Second Brain:
Empowering health through the gut 68

Walking into Confidence:
Eyes open, standing and walking meditation 70

Locating Your Power: *Release anxiety and reclaim your identity*

You were born with a strong life force within you, and as you have grown and matured you have been given the free will to use that life force to make your own decisions and to find your own path. This includes the people you have chosen to be friends with, maybe for a short while or for your entire life, the sports you chose to participate in at school, to the foods you choose to eat or not eat, the hobbies you have, the people you engage in relationships with, what you do for work, and what you do on your weekends. These all come down to your free will, your desire, your passion, what you love, and what you believe. You have always and will continue to define your own identity, and that is what makes us all so wonderfully unique.

When we think of the word "power," it might instantly make us think of someone or something outside of us, an individual or a group of people. Someone seemingly in a position of power: our politicians, our boss at work, the police, the army, or world leaders. Sometimes you may feel like you have no power and you are just a puppet, and that someone else has hold of the strings.

**THIRD ENERGY CENTER/
YELLOW WHEEL OF LIGHT ENERGY**
Associations: Confidence, willpower, health

For me, my power comes from my integrity, the feeling that I'm being authentic to who I really want to be and to what I know to be true in my mind and heart, the awareness that I'm aligned with it all, and of course having fun along the way! That makes me feel confident and sure. It is a "knowing," deep within my belly. Have you felt that too?

In this Locating your Power meditation we will work with the third energy center in our bodies. This is located at the solar plexus and is in the space 2 inches (5 centimeters) above the belly button and underneath and behind your front lower ribs (see page 18). Its color is yellow. Spend a moment reading each step, and then allow yourself to spend some time in each step with your eyes closed before moving onto the next.

INTENTION

I locate my power and reignite my will and passion.

MEDITATION (FOR AUDIO VERSION SEE PAGE 140)

1. Find a comfortable space, either sitting or lying down. Feel your spine lengthen and your shoulders soften.

2. Take a moment here to relax and with three slow, cleansing breaths, settle the monkey mind (see page 23). As you breathe, feel a sense of peace and serenity wash throughout your entire torso.

3. Now take your attention directly to your solar plexus. If you wish, place your palm flat on this space. Breathe deeply and feel completely centered with every breath.

4. Begin to feel and visualize a warm yellow glow like the sunshine, a vibrant ball of yellow light or energy, right in the center of the solar plexus. Does this light spin like a wheel, does it flicker, does it pulsate?

5. Continue to focus upon the light until you feel it begin to become steady and strong. With its strength it begins to expand out in all directions, emanating past the walls of your body until you are completely encapsulated and illuminated within this ball of yellow, glowing energy—a field of light energy around you.

6. Feel the power and strength from this light right there from its source, the solar plexus.

7. Bring to mind the word "YES," and feel the word YES within this color. YES yellow light. YES to my Power.

8. Consider the following, taking about one to two minutes on each point.

What does it feel like to feel steady and sure?

What does it feel like to have a strong will?

What does it feel like to feel passionate for life?

What does it feel like to be authentic to yourself and to your identity?

9. Finish with the following affirmations. Repeat each affirmation three times as you focus on that third energy center.

I accept myself exactly the way I am.

I am proud of myself.

I recognize I am strong and powerful.

I am enough.

I am empowered.

Yes!

Jai, Namaste.

Note: *Jai* means "Victory."

Your Confident Body: *Feeling great in the skin you're in and trusting your body*

You may be the sort of person who tends to take your body for granted and not give it much attention at all, until perhaps it fails you and cries out for help due to illness. I've heard it said that you never fully appreciate being able to breathe until you get a cold, you have a blocked-up nose, and you can't anymore. Isn't that the truth! Alternatively, you might be the sort of person who obsesses about your body and health so much that it takes up every waking minute of your time with over-thinking.

Science tells us that what we tell ourselves, and what we think, feel, and do has a direct impact on how our body responds, the way it feels, and believe it or not the way it looks.

Comparing our bodies to others and not feeling good about our bodies are big issues in this day and age. They can lead some people down the slippery path of body dysmorphia, obsessing over tiny flaws as the image in the mirror becomes distorted. Yet what is seen in the mirror is not an accurate image of what the person actually looks like.

When we are unhappy with our body, weight, or level of attractiveness it can trigger a stress response within us. This can affect our wellbeing, our energy levels, and our self-esteem.

Meditation can help us to reprogram negative thought patterns and help us to feel whole so that we can enjoy our bodies again. In this meditation we will work with ideas of kindness and respect for our wonderful bodies and practice gratitude. Refer back to the magnificence of your body in Your Powerful Body (see page 18). Let this time be just for you. It is a time to switch off from the pressures of the outside world and social media and reconnect with your miraculous, confident body.

Learn to love yourself again.

As you follow the meditation, read step 1, and then close your eyes and do the step before moving on to step 2 and so on.

INTENTION
Today I celebrate my body. My body is worthy of my care and I will look after it.

MEDITATION (FOR AUDIO VERSION SEE PAGE 140)

1. Begin either sitting or lying down, however you feel most comfortable. Let your awareness draw inward.

2. Bring your attention to your entire body with some opening, cleansing breaths. As you inhale, squeeze up your body super tight and tense, and as you exhale let the body go slack and relaxed. Repeat this three times.

3. Now... be still. Allow your body to breathe by itself. There is no need to control it— allow the process of respiration to happen naturally and effortlessly, as an easy in and easy out. If you are comfortable to do so, bring the lips together and breathe exclusively through the nose.

4. Now bring your attention to the mind and let go of critical thoughts and conversations with others or yourself. Feel your mind soften and expand a little in the space.

5. Feel the brain within your skull. Feel the left hemisphere, feel the right hemisphere. As you breathe, let the brain relax. Practice gratitude for all the functions of the brain: your memory, initiating and controlling movement, interpreting your senses. Be grateful for your brain.

6. Bring your attention to your lungs. Experience the breath moving in and out. Feel grateful for your respiratory system that guides fresh air and oxygen into your body as you inhale and removes waste gases from the body as you exhale. This is a process of exchange that happens thousands of times a day without you even having to think about it. Be grateful for your lungs.

7. Shift your attention now to the heart, which beats in rhythm in the chest providing a pump to send oxygen and nutrient-rich blood to all parts of your body, into every single cell. Be grateful for your heart.

8. Your attention once again shifts, now to the stomach and all areas of the digestive system, which processes every item of nutritious food you eat, drawing from it the correct vitamins and nutrients to create vital proteins and energy. Your body does incredible things on a day-to-day basis. Be grateful for your entire body.

9. Also acknowledge your arms, legs, hands, and feet, and all the intricate things they aid you to do each and every single day.

10. Notice if any feelings come up about your body at this time and just be curious about them. Even if they are negative, don't judge yourself, just accept that these are feelings you are having right now.

11. Repeat silently to yourself the following:

I forgive my body for its pain.

My body is worthy of my care and I will love and look after it and be kind to it.

I accept this body that I have.

I breathe deep so that my body can enjoy the energy the breath brings.

I am grateful for my body's strength and resilience.

My body is capable of incredible things.

12. With your next few breaths, spend a few moments connecting with this practice and thinking of your own ways to be kinder to yourself (see the suggestions below). Gift yourself this time. Remember that when you feel good your body releases good hormones and you will SPARKLE and GLOW.

Ways to be kinder to yourself

You could drink a little more water each day, get to bed earlier or wake up a little earlier, go to yoga or an exercise class, feel good as you move your body, meditate daily, read a book, go for a run or to the gym, practice relaxation techniques, book a massage, wear warmer clothes or cooler clothes, wear comfortable clothes and shoes. And definitely engage in more positive self-talk.

The Second Brain: *Empowering health through the gut*

A "gut feeling" is the feeling you get in your gut about something; you just don't know why or how you know it, but it's deep, visceral, and unmistakable. This feeling often comes with some sort of sensation, such as butterflies, cramps, a tightness, a rumbling, or perhaps even just a feeling of absolute clarity. We might say "I don't know, it doesn't feel right in my gut," or "My gut is telling me that I should/should not."

It's no coincidence that scientists call our gut our second brain. And although it doesn't read Shakespeare or attempt mental arithmetic, it does contain over 100 million brain cells (neurons). We spoke in the section on balance about the mind-body connection and how our body is in constant communication with the brain (see page 42). Not only does your gut send signals to the brain to tell it that it is hungry, it also has the ability to feel when something is or isn't right. It's also interesting to discover that stomach problems are the most common symptoms of stress, anxiety, and depression.

Let's treat our gut with the respect it deserves, not only by nourishing it with nutritious food, but also by bringing our attention and energy to it and our third energy center (see page 18) in this meditation. We will fill it with radiant light, begin the process of dissolving any unwanted tension or emotions that have got stuck, and begin to empower it with the magic of our second brain.

INTENTION
I visualize a beautiful yellowy golden light energy like the sun soothing my gut.

MEDITATION (FOR AUDIO VERSION SEE PAGE 140)

1. Sit in a way that feels steady and comfortable for you.

2. Roll your shoulders backward three times and forward three times. Stretch out your neck to the right and left, or move in any way you feel you need to in order to ease tension and tightness in the upper body.

3. Place your palms flat onto the solar plexus (see page 18), with your hands one on top of the other, and begin to take deep breaths into the hands. With every breath, feel the hands expand as you bring life and energy to that area.

4. Notice for any sensations within the stomach, any tightness or pain, perhaps a sense of butterflies. Is the sensation you feel linked to any particular emotion, worry, guilt, anxiety, stress, anger, or depression? If you can't feel anything at all, that's completely fine, just keep breathing into this space.

5. Notice the intensity of any emotion whether it is in the stomach or wherever it may exist within the body. Visualize it like hard jagged rocks wherever it is.

6. Reconnect with your deeper breath and feel it deeply balancing and melting the hard rocks. They melt like fudge or butter, turning from a hard solid to a soft liquid. The liquid is not sticky; it dissolves and flows away.

7. Continue this process for as long as you need to, using your complete focus and concentration. Recognize any emotion or tightness, feeling it like hard rocks and then use the breath to help it change density and eventually vanish.

8. Notice the freedom that you feel once the tightness and stress have dissolved away. And begin to draw a beautiful golden, yellow, light energy in from the sun. Feel the sunbeams entering into your solar plexus and soothing, softening, cleansing, cleaning, and creating space for your life force and creative energy.

9. Let the sunshine in your belly begin to beam and radiate out of the stomach, illuminating the world around you. Feel it energizing you, enhancing the processes of the digestive system so that they work at maximum efficiency, empowering the army of your immune system to fight illness and disease.

10. Feel dynamic. Feel strong. Feel unlimited.

11. Stay here as long as you need to and continue to bring ideas of strength, creativity, and wholeness to mind. When you're ready you can open your eyes.

Be receptive—Namaste.

Walking into Confidence: *Eyes open, standing and walking meditation*

This meditation is the first of two standing and moving meditations in this book. Learning to meditate with your eyes open while you are walking is powerful, as it will enable you to tap into the tool and power of meditation at any given time. Once you are familiar with this meditation, you'll be able to tune into the benefits while you walk to work, to the store, out in nature, or wherever you wish. Notice how the way you walk changes and uplifts your energy and confidence.

Always practice this meditation in an area of land where you feel safe, so in your back yard if you have one, a local park, or out in the countryside—somewhere where you can be safe and undisturbed. My partner and I always practice walking meditations when we are on vacation. We wake up early to catch the sunrise, feel the sun powering up our cells, and walk along the beach, through the resort, or through a nearby pine forest. Not only is it an excellent way to start the day, we also get to explore through our meditation with a calm peaceful gaze and end up feeling empowered and energized for the day ahead.

Read the following instructions carefully so you don't get confused when you start the actual meditation. There is a bit of "business" to get to grips with.

You will begin standing still with your eyes open, then you will be instructed to close the eyes, and after a while you will be instructed to open the eyes for the walking section of the meditation. We will then end the meditation once again standing still with our eyes closed. Use your meditation to practice your confidence not only with your eyes closed, but also with your eyes open and walking.

INTENTION
I am magnificent.

MEDITATION (FOR AUDIO VERSION SEE PAGE 140)

1. Start standing, with your feet hip width apart, your knees soft, and your arms hanging loose by your sides. Have your eyes open and gaze out to the horizon in front of you. A steady gaze, a calm gaze, a relaxed gaze.

2. Take a nice deep inhale and hold it at the top... and then as you exhale relax your entire body. Feel your body standing here and relax it deeply. Take in your entire surroundings. What can you see? What can you smell? What can you hear? What can you feel on your skin? Take another inhale and hold it and as you exhale allow the eyes to gently close.

3. Focus your attention on the connection between your feet and the ground beneath you. As you press down into the earth, the taller you feel your body become. Take a breath into that, and inhale and feel how strong, sure, and steady you are, then hold it, and exhale and relax.

4. Spread the toes and firmly root the soles deep into the earth. Feel the feet drawing energy from the earth beneath you and up into the legs and lower body, noticing the sensations in your body. Feel that energy moving up through the abdomen, tingling through the whole of the torso, down both the arms to the fingers, up through the neck, head, brain, and out of the crown of the head.

5. One more time as you inhale this time from the feet, feel the energy rising right up the body to the crown... hold it, and relax your body and feel your body relax... relax it even more and then exhale and release.

6. Now become aware of the infinite space above, in front, behind, and all around you. How deep does the endless space go? Breathe into that space, and feel and sense into that space. How deep can your awareness go? Let the energy of your body dissolve into the energy of the space around you. Float your awareness out deep into space, among the stars and the planets.

7. Bring your attention to your brain. Breathe into your brain. Long slow breaths.

8. Bring your attention to your heart. Breathe into your heart. Long slow breaths.

Be passionate.

Be magnificent.

Be the person you really want to be.

Overcome your past and anything that has held you back.

Release any chains and attachment.

Feel your heart opening to love.

Feel your mind open to possibility and opportunity.

As your energy changes, so do you; stronger, more confident, more empowered.

9. Bring your attention to your solar plexus, then to your third energy center in the body (see page 18). Cultivate feelings of empowerment, confidence, free will, strength, love, and determination.

10. Now open your eyes, expand your awareness, and breathe into it... begin to shift your weight from one foot to the other, then when you are ready, begin to walk. Walk into confidence. Feel the life force that is within you. Feel the solid earth beneath each footstep.

11. Pick up the pace and walk at a speed that feels most authentic and appropriate for you. Find a rhythm and a beat to your walk. What does your confident walk feel like? Hold your head up high and walk as a powerful being. Fill your entire body with the energy of confidence.

12. Begin to slow down your walk and as you come to stand still, bring your hands to your heart and close your eyes once more. Take a breath; you're here now. Feel gratitude and open yourself up to change, to confidence, to connection, to clear expression, to creation, to appreciation, to expansion, to a deeper discovery—to a more powerful you. Breathe into this a new energy.

And when you're ready, open your eyes and come back the transformed you, taking this mindful awareness into your day.

Chapter Four

Connection

Through technology and social media, we are more connected than ever before.

When I was a child, I remember my mother telling me that one day in the future there would be a screen on our home phone that would enable me to see as well as talk to my Nana and Grandad. I was amazed just by that thought! We lived in Manchester and my grandparents lived in Wales in the UK—so a mere 200 miles away—but it meant a car journey that seemed to take an entire day on busy English motorways (freeways). In those days we had a home phone attached by a cord to the wall in our hallway and we'd sit on the stairs to have our conversations. Cell phones were a new thing and were the size of a brick. Only businessmen had them and they carried them around in boxes. This was only 30 years ago... how far we have come! We are more connected via our devices now than ever before. If I, for example, want to see my family in Australia I just pick up my cell phone (which is rarely more than a few feet away from me), call for free, and I can see their smiling faces, watch my beautiful nieces growing up, and share special moments, connecting in a much deeper way.

In a world where we are seemingly so connected with each other, why do we feel so disconnected from ourselves?

While technology and social media have their many benefits, there is so much to do and so many moving parts to keep up with that it's fair to say that we can all sometimes feel a little overwhelmed. Keeping up with developments in AI and the next new gadgets and apps, answering endless text messages and emails, and the comparison trap of the hundreds of new social media platforms... it can all feel like an immense strain, leaving very little time for our brains and hearts to just be still. Add this to a busy work schedule and it can easily lead to stress, burn-out, anxiety, or even depression.

Reconnecting with yourself through meditative practices such as the ones in this book, can help you to build your resilience and discover that happiness, strength, and support starting from within and not outside ourselves. This is important for not only our mental and physical health but also our emotional and spiritual wellbeing. When you can deeply connect to yourself and care more about how you feel on a day-to-day basis, you are more inclined to seek out activities and relationships that make you feel good and enhance your life. Connection is a cure and contributes to us feeling greater love and appreciation for everything in our lives. So let's begin to connect to our beautiful hearts, allowing ourselves to process life more efficiently and uplift our energy.

Meditations in this chapter

Breathing Heart: *Calm stress and reset*

The first meditation of this chapter is very simple yet profoundly effective. I have used it for many years and it always makes me feel better in times of stress.

The heart is deeply intelligent. It has its own nervous system and is constantly exchanging information with the brain. The heart also has an ability to feel. For example, we can feel nourishing feelings of love or painful feelings of heartbreak and loss. Breathing into your heart space creates a soothing effect, especially when you use uplifting emotions to do so. Since the heart and brain are constantly communicating, when we soothe our heart through this meditation we will also soothe our brain.

This meditation is excellent for any time of day, wherever you are. Read each step and then practice eyes open or closed for a few minutes until you begin to feel a shift in your energy.

INTENTION

I connect to my heartbeat and breathe purely for a sense of relaxation. I experience my energy rise, and feel my insides sparkle.

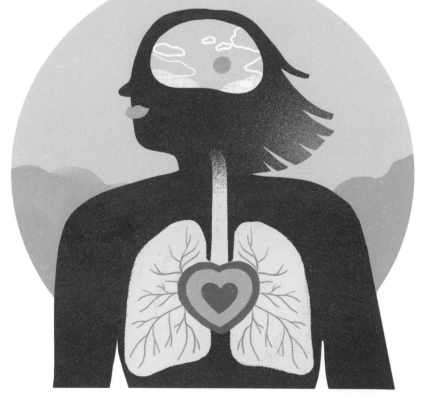

MEDITATION (FOR AUDIO VERSION SEE PAGE 141)

1. Be completely relaxed. You can practice this anywhere, alone or in the presence of others, eyes open or closed, sitting, standing, or walking.

2. Bring the whole of your awareness to your heart. Imagine that your breath is flowing in through the heart and flowing out through the heart. Breathe more slowly, deeply, and expansively than before. Allow a few moments or minutes.

3. Think of an uplifting feeling or emotion that you have for someone or something. For example: love, appreciation, kindness, passion, happiness, joy, or something else that makes you feel really good. As you continue breathing through the heart, bring to mind that emotion and observe how it feels within your heart as you think about it. Spend as long as you wish here.

4. Now imagine sending that feeling out into the world, radiating a beam of love and light energy out to others and also back into your own heart. Use whatever imagery that comes to mind. Feel the energy and the power, and experience the impact this has on your heart.

5. Continue to carry this experience with you into the rest of your day.

Be receptive—Namaste.

**FOURTH ENERGY CENTER/
GREEN WHEEL OF LIGHT ENERGY**
Associations: Love, compassion, respect

The Inner-Ease™ Technique from HeartMath®

The practice of the Inner-Ease™ technique was developed by HeartMath® (see page 15) and is one of my favorite techniques to help you to reconnect to your heart. It can be used anytime, anywhere, in any situation with your eyes open or closed. The Inner-Ease™ tool is something that you can use and practice even without anyone noticing you are doing it...

You might say, it's like a top-secret super power!

This tool is different to all the other practices in this book, in that it is not meditation but a technique. In meditation we mostly have our eyes closed and our focus directed either inwardly or outwardly, on whatever we are meditating upon in that moment. But with the HeartMath® techniques, the focus can be on whatever you are doing at the time, and also upon your breath and the most powerful organ in the body, your heart. I find this practice to be magical.

HeartMath® techniques help you to quickly change your state, from stressed-out to calm in a matter of seconds or minutes.

You could practice Inner-Ease™ while you're driving in your car, engaging in conversation, or operating on someone in the ER. You could be fighting a fire or in a war zone, a crowd of people, or any situation where you'd like to feel more resilient, rational, and coherent.

In Inner-Ease™ you are connecting seamlessly to your heart. Heartmath's incredible research has claimed that over 1,400 biological markers within the body will change and up-regulate. This can bring

about improvements in focus and concentration, a stronger immune system. It can also slow down bio markers reflective in the ageing process, reduce inflammation in the body, and help fight disease. You can read more about this in the research papers published at www.heartmath.org.

I use Inner-Ease™ most days, but especially when traveling on public transport around the busy city of London. I'll tell you a story... I first noticed my heart rate was high when I used to walk from my home to the bus stop on my way to work. Occasionally if I was late I'd run for the bus, which naturally as you would expect caused my heart rate to rise and signaled a stress response in my body.

However, I began to discover that even when I wasn't in a rush, my heart rate was still increasing as a kind of memorized response to the simple act of walking to the bus stop. I realized that during those times I had been rushing, I had practiced a "stressed-out, anxious, I'm late feeling," and so even when I wasn't stressed or late my body was having the same familiar heightened reaction. My body couldn't tell the difference anymore—I was on autopilot!

Inner-Ease™ will bring the heart into coherence and you into a state of balance and flow. Your mind and emotions will become synchronized with one another, so that you can stay calm, focused, and alert in any situation. The instructions are extremely simple, and you can spend a minute or two on each step or longer as you wish.

The Inner-Ease™ Technique (For audio version see page 141)

1. Focus your attention on the heart. Imagine your breath flowing in and out of the heart or chest area, and breathe a little slower and deeper than usual. Suggestion: Inhale for five seconds and exhale for five seconds or whatever is comfortable.

2. With each breath draw in a feeling of inner ease to balance your mental and emotional energy.

3. Set a meaningful intention to anchor the feeling of inner ease as you engage in your projects, challenges, and daily interactions.

Expand Your Relationships: *Unconditional love*

You are your NUMBER ONE priority. This statement might sound selfish. But there is absolutely nothing selfish about giving yourself time every day to do what you need to do, so that you feel confident enough, positive enough, vibrant enough, and energized enough to shine your light onto everyone you meet. This is why you must be your number one priority above anyone else, and yes that means even before your children and most certainly before your lover and friends. This twisted my brain for many years before I fully understood what it means to be unconditional in love. Bear with me on this...

You are worthy of your love and care.

Making yourself a priority is crucial for building a healthy, fulfilling life and strong, loving connections with others. When you prioritize your own needs, you are better equipped to show up for others and love them unconditionally. For me this means a yoga and meditation practice every morning. This is a non-negotiable for me in my relationships whether I'm at home with my partner, visiting family or friends, away on a work trip, or on vacation; I always make time for my meditation practice as I know it makes me feel fantastic! Other things important for me are meeting up with my friends for brunch, taking trips to the theater, and going for long walks in the English countryside with my partner and dog at the weekends. These things really put the juice in my battery!

What recharges you? Take time to write a few things down so that you can ensure you plot them into your schedule often.

Every single day, when I have completed my meditation, my energy is present, calm, and stable. I've dredged out the majority of my negativity and morning anxiety, my battery is once again full, and I'm ready to show up for the people in my life with a smile on my face and a positive outlook. I find it also sets a good example for others and empowers them to do the same. If we don't allow ourselves the time to do what we need to do to show up as the best version of ourselves, that can be a disservice to others. Do you see now how being your own number one priority is not at all selfish? Remember, self-love and unconditional love go hand in hand. So make yourself a priority, and watch as your relationships flourish and thrive.

Unconditional love is a powerful, magical force that can transform our lives and the world around us. It is a type of love that is not based on conditions or expectations, but rather a deep acceptance and appreciation for ourselves and others. Rather than asking or needing people to be, feel, or act a certain way, you allow them to be their authentic selves and shine love over them regardless. This doesn't mean that you're a doormat and allow people to mistreat you—we still must seek loving boundaries. It means you are not dependent on their behavior in order to feel good. You just feel good anyway. When we cultivate a practice of unconditional love, we open ourselves up to greater compassion, empathy, and deeper connections with those around us and ensure that we only attract the best relationships and experiences into our lives.

This meditation will guide you to build up your own power and then to explore and experience the transformative power of unconditional love within yourself and toward others.

INTENTION

I feel good and love unconditionally—love is my truth, love is all there is.

MEDITATION (FOR AUDIO VERSION SEE PAGE 141)

1. Come to your favorite seated meditation position. Allow yourself to be still and your arms and hands to rest in your lap. Become aware of your natural breath. Don't try to control it, just be present and enjoy it.

2. As you close the eyes, gently move the attention into a place within you. The worries of the world around you fall away; they fall off the right side of your body and off the left side of your body, and both the shoulders relax.

3. The skull balances on top of your straight spine and all features of the face soften and relax inward. The forehead, eyebrows, eyeballs, eyelids, eyelashes are all soft. The nose relaxes. Let go of the cheeks and feel all tension dissolve from the jaw, so there is a gap between your upper and lower teeth. The tongue rests lightly on the roof of the mouth. And there is a gentle, serene smile upon your face.

4. Let your attention go directly to the right side of your physical heart. Breathe deeply into that space. Imagine a small crescent shape just resting easy and gently on the right side of your physical heart. At this crescent space, everything is perfect. The crescent glows like the beautiful moon and is as bright as the stars. Here the divine self resides, here everything is completely peaceful, safe, and calm; it is pure love and completely whole.

5. As your heart begins to open you may begin to feel the warm glow. The color of this energy center is green. Visualize a wheel of green energy soothing and loving through the heart. Ask yourself right now if there is anything the heart wants you to know. Don't worry if words don't come to you right away, just listen and see if it can offer you any words of wisdom. Spend as much time here as you need.

6. Let this warm loving light glow deeply into every cell of your entire body. Send deep appreciation and gratitude to yourself for this time to connect.

7. Now begin to send this glowing light outward, let it connect with the light of someone in your life. Visualize that person and appreciate them for the experiences or lessons they have provided you in life. These could be happy or sad lessons. Perhaps lessons that have caused you to evolve and grow, to get clear on your path, to help you understand what you don't want, or to help you understand what you do want. A person you love, or who loves you. A person who has challenged or inspired you. It could be a friend, a family member, or a colleague. This could be a person who you see often or rarely, it could be someone that is no longer with us in physical form. Hold that person's image firmly in your mind and feel your appreciation for them. If it helps, imagine a memory of them from the past.

Visualize them in their strongest situation—healthy, relaxed, and spirited with a big smile upon their face.

8. Magnetize the image of them deep into your heart. Imagine you are placing their perfect heart into yours.

9. Feel the breath moving in and out of your heart center. Let your breath intensify your feelings of love and empower the energy of your heart. Fill up your heart and their heart with this love. Their heart nestled inside yours.

Breathe in love and exhale out a bright light. Let a little more love into your heart.

10. Stay connected to your breath and come back to the image of the person. Visualize that you can also see your heart is inside their heart, feel their connection. Everything is perfect.

Breathe in light and exhale out love. Feel deep love in the heart.

11. Notice the unconditional love that you have flowing with abundance out to all people around you and feel it being returned directly back to you.

Keep focusing on the energy of love.

12. Now place a hand on your heart and let all hearts become one, always connected in love. Keep in mind that love is not something you have to look for... it is something that is deep inside of you every moment of every day. And when you are ready you can open your eyes.

Be receptive—Namaste.

Love Beyond Time: *A meditation to help overcome grief*

Grief and loss are a natural and inevitable part of our human experience that we will all go through at numerous stages in our lives. Whether a loved one has passed away, or we are grieving the loss of a relationship, have experienced a major life change, or are simply feeling overwhelmed by the world around us, grief can feel extremely difficult to navigate.

Deeper connection.

While it can be a painful and challenging process, grief is also an opportunity for growth, healing, and even deeper connection with ourselves and others. Although it feels like an ending, it is also a beginning and can be the start of an exciting new chapter in your life journey.

Even though you may feel heartbroken, remind yourself that a heart cannot actually break. There is no single way to heal grief and many people have their own individual ways, but by honoring our grief we can cultivate self-compassion and find some comfort in the present moment. Although it can feel scary, it's important to take the time to acknowledge and sit with our grief so that we can begin to process our emotions and find a sense of peace amidst the pain.

This meditation is like a big heart hug. You will learn to navigate the complexities of grief with greater ease, finding moments of calm and clarity.

INTENTION
I invite my heart to be nourished, soothed, and taken care of.
I feel a big heart hug!

MEDITATION (FOR AUDIO VERSION SEE PAGE 141)

1. Lie down or sit comfortably in a place where you feel safe to let go. Be soft and gentle with yourself. Move slowly until you are comfortable. As you close your eyes, bring yourself into this present moment and breathe more slowly and deeply than before.

2. Begin by placing your hands over your beautiful heart. Lengthen and deepen your breath, sending each breath into your hands and deep into your heart's space.

3. Let all your attention gently move to the heart.

4. Allow the heart to simply feel any pain, any ache, any sorrow, any deep grief; it is all okay. You might feel fearful and scared to actually let your emotions out, but remind yourself you are safe and supported right here, right now.

5. If at any point you feel the urge to deeply sigh, or even let out any noise or sounds, perhaps if you feel you want to sob or cry, that is also totally okay.

6. What emotions are you feeling? If you can name the emotion, then whisper it to yourself—"sadness," "despair," "loss," anything at all. It's important to feel. Continue to breathe.

Allow the energy of sadness to release outward, allow all emotion to flow.

Continue to breathe, letting your breath anchor you at this difficult time.

7. Notice your hands again protecting your heart, offering healing through your hands. This meditation is a big heart hug. Send deep love and care to yourself at this difficult time. Stay here as long as you need.

8. When you feel the energy, tightness, or pain beginning to become softer here, then scan your body for any other points of tightness. Perhaps your throat, or your stomach, lower abdomen, shoulders, or brain.

9. Allow your hands or just your attention to move into those points of tightness to offer healing and support. Continue to focus on the sensation of energy in this place—it may escalate and get stronger at first. Continue to focus until you feel a release. Spend as long as you need here.

10. Close your meditation with a deep sense of gratitude to yourself. Firstly for your ability to heal and process, for the time spent to honor your emotions, and for the capacity you have for deep love and care. You are incredible. Silently to yourself say thank you three times...

Thank you, thank you, thank you.

11. Let yourself now slowly move out of your meditation. Continue to be gentle with yourself. Now perhaps it's time to move back into your day, take a nap, or drift off to sleep. Allow yourself to continue to rest and rebuild your strength.

Be receptive—Namaste.

Chapter Five

Expression

Expression is a vital aspect of all human communication and connection.

Expression is our ability to convey our feelings and ideas through various mediums such as speech, writing, dance/movement, art, and music. It enables us to share our unique perspectives, experiences, and emotions with the world.

Having the ability to express clearly is crucial for...

- Personal and spiritual growth

- Building empathy and relationships

- Encouraging a more inclusive and compassionate society

It is essential to encourage and support our friends, family, and everyone we meet to express themselves freely and authentically so that they can feel a greater sense of creativity, self-awareness, vitality, and purpose. Freedom of expression has been important to me from a young age and still feels vital to this present day. As a child I was deeply shy and would freeze even when a teacher was taking the register/roll call in the morning. I found it so hard to answer "Yes Sir/Miss" out loud. My mom taught me to take a deep breath and be brave.

Odd as it may seem, I then found myself drawn to singing and dancing, which I did all through my childhood and eventually as a profession on stage around the world and in the West End in London. I loved being able to convey emotion through dance and make the audience think through the plays and stories I could tell from the stage. Being myself in a normal setting was much harder than being on the stage. Even though I was a seemingly confident actor, I really had to practice being myself! As a result nobody I met and none of my friends would say I was shy—I could hide it well.

Although I could hide my shyness, I had issues around my throat—a blockage of energy I suppose. This would manifest itself as hoarseness, laryngitis, tonsillitis, glandular fever, and acid reflux intermittently throughout my twenties and into my early thirties until I learned how to release the energy in that area. I'm convinced my daily meditation practice cured my sometimes debilitating acid reflux. Even now if something has deeply upset me—a grief or a loss—the pain in my throat is like knives. Through meditation and allowing myself to surrender, I have learned to soothe that area. It is constant "work in progress," but I now feel much more freedom and no longer suffer physical unease (dis-ease) in my throat.

As a teacher of the spiritual arts and a voiceover actor today, my voice plays a crucial role in everything I do, and I feel that my confident expression is thanks to some of the following meditations. Whether you have a blockage in your throat like I did or elsewhere in the body, you will learn the technique of release, and empower your ability to express. We begin by letting go and then we will connect to a "clear vision" so that we can express our creativity and desired reality.

Meditations in this chapter

Letting Go: *Bright white skeleton meditation for release*

Letting go can be difficult, but it is a necessary practice for our mental and emotional wellbeing. It requires us to release our attachment to things that no longer serve us, such as negative thoughts, past experiences, or unfulfilling relationships. The Buddha taught us that..."the root of all suffering is attachment." To truly understand this concept, first just take a look at yourself in the mirror. Every day you change a little bit, every day you grow older, every day you learn something new and are constantly changing, as is everything else and everyone else in the universe. Change is an essential process of life; we learn, we evolve, and we expand on our path to growth.

Letting go is release and it is freedom from whatever we are holding on to.

In the first section, Presence, and the meditation Cycles of Life: Connecting in nature (see page 34), we explored the theory that everything has a "life cycle"—a birth, a life, and then a death. As our life changes through its own cycle, there will constantly be loss and rebirth and loss again. Birth and death are in fact all around us every day of our lives— just take a look at the seasons. We've also just explored grief in the previous section, Connection. So we are well aware of the pain involved in losing something that we've really loved. This is often something that we have grown attached to. We feel this grief maybe as pain, heartache, or some other physical unease (dis-ease) within the body, until we can learn to soften it and let go of our tight grip on the past.

FIFTH ENERGY CENTER/BLUE WHEEL OF LIGHT ENERGY
Associations: Truth, freedom, empowerment

When we let go, it allows energy and life force within us to move, but it also allows the constant flow of the entire universe. Letting go can be painful, and so often we may not want to let go so we can avoid confronting our pain. We may even deliberately choose to avoid our thoughts, feelings, and emotions—this is called suppression. It is a conscious choice to not deal with our problems. We just build up our walls or pretend it's not there.

We may also store pain and stress within our body unconsciously—this is called repression. You may have tension or pain and you can't figure out why. But don't worry, the good news is that you don't have to know the exact reasons behind the pain you feel to be able to let go. You just need to be able to feel the sensation and frequency of the energy and focus upon it until it begins to become less.

Where can pain become trapped within the body?

It is well documented that our emotional responses stay logged in the body anywhere you either consciously or unconsciously store your emotion. As I discussed in the introduction to this chapter, I felt a lot of tightness in my throat—you may often have heard people say the phrase, "I have a lump in my throat." For me this was caused by deeply unconscious feelings of doubt, under confidence, and worry. You might have also heard people say "I feel that within my gut," "I've got a gut-wrenching feeling," or "I've got

butterflies in my belly." Unprocessed energy in the gut can lead to ailments such as ulcers or irritable bowel syndrome. We can also feel tightness in our shoulders, lower back, hips, or anywhere. The tightness or pain is energy bound up around itself. Rather than energy flowing like a wave, it is circling and causing emotion to be trapped and tangled.

Through meditation, we can learn to observe all attachments without judgment and cultivate the ability to let them go. Remember the word meditation means "to become familiar with." If we can locate the pain within the body and focus on the energy of the pain, we will eventually feel it dissolve and release. This can feel a little scary at first. But trust the process and continue to acknowledge and release these experiences and sensations. By doing so, we can create space for new experiences and positive growth in our lives.

This meditation is a version of a Buddhist meditation which is designed to promote healing and surrendering of trapped energy and pain. It involves picturing a skeleton. We all know roughly what our skeleton looks like, but if you need to, google it to remind yourself. It's important to be able to visualize as many bones as you can, so it's always helpful to have a picture handy.

INTENTION

In letting go there should be no effort—so I truly relax, surrender, and let my energy flow.

MEDITATION (FOR AUDIO VERSION SEE PAGE 141)

1. Lie down in your bed so that you are completely at ease. Feel the density of your body, and its weight into the mattress, allowing it to completely sink and surrender more deeply so that you feel peaceful in your personal space. Allow your eyelids to gently close.

2. Feel the joints in the ankles, knees, and hips and relax them. Feel the joints of the wrists, elbows, and shoulders and relax them.

3. Bring your attention to your breath and then take three deep, slow breaths using the following instructions. Every time you inhale slowly and deeply, squeeze the body as tight as you can. Squeeze your fingers into your palms, squeeze the muscles of your arms, point and squeeze the feet, squeeze the muscles of your legs, buttocks, the muscles of your belly, and face. Squeeze and hold everything very tightly. Then as you exhale, let all the muscles release, relax, and go soft. Repeat three times.

Relax, relax, relax, and allow your body to once again become still and heavy.

4. Now continue to breathe in through the nose and out through the nose, in a rhythm that feels most natural for you. Imagine your breath moving into your entire body, right down the legs into the toes, right down the arms and into the fingers and thumbs, and up into the brain, the right side of the brain, the left side of the brain.

5. Observe any tightness, tension, or pain within your physical body—any place you are holding on. Perhaps an emotion remains stuck within the body. What is it? Doubt, guilt, frustration, disappointment, anger, or something else? Can you label it? If you can, then say it quietly to yourself and focus upon it. If you can't label the emotion then just stay with the sensation. Spend as long here as you need to and really feel what it is you'd like to let go of. Feel the tension as energy... it may heighten but slowly it will begin to decrease.

Follow the next few steps with your imagination. Let it guide you into a deep sense of bliss, surrender, and freedom.

6. Visualize all the flesh, muscles, and organs dissolving away from your bones, and with that dissolving they take away your stress, tension, pain, and discomfort or "dis-ease." Allow your skin, tissues, and fibers

to melt... and completely vanish, leaving behind only your body's skeleton.

7. Bring your attention to the feet—there are 26 bones in each foot. Imagine each one of these bones glowing a bright white healing light. Feel the healing energy of this light. Imagine the ankles, lower legs, and knee bones, all of them glowing a bright white healing light. Continue into the upper legs, hips, and the large pelvic bone, all glowing a bright white light.

8. Feel the healing energy from the tips of the toes right up the legs to the hip bones.

9. Now visualize each of the 33 bones/vertebrae of the spine, like a string of fairy lights, each individual vertebrae a bright white healing light. The light floods through the ribs wrapping from the back to the front, up through the breast bone, a bright white healing light.

10. Bright white light infuses the collar bones and goes down the shoulders into the shoulder blades. Right down the upper arms to the elbows, imagine the bones the best you can, as a bright white healing light. The light continues to the lower arms, wrists, and to the 27 individual bones that make up each of the hands. Feel the bright white healing light right into the tips of the fingers and thumbs.

11. Finally bring your attention to the skull. Imagine it as a bright white healing light. Feel it and enjoy it.

> *The whole skeleton glows brightly: illuminated, pure, and energized.*

12. Now it's time to rebuild the flesh body—how would you want your body to feel? How would you want your body to look? Build yourself a healthy, strong, and peaceful yet powerful body from the feet and legs, reconstructing the flesh and the muscles. Continuing up the torso, the main trunk of the body, strong healthy organs, now through the arms and hands, reconstructing the flesh, the muscles. Then rebuild the features of the face so they are just the way you want them. Even rebuild your beautiful brain, a mind of pure clarity, unlimited energy, and a sense of freedom.

13. Be grateful for your powerful body and a vibrant, fresh, sparkly energy.

14. When you are ready you can wiggle your toes, your fingers, your nose, and finally you can open your eyes.

Be receptive—Namaste.

Finding Your Voice: *Speak your truth*

Finding your own authentic voice and speaking the truth about what you truly want, need, and desire in life can be a difficult and interesting voyage and may require a lot of patience with yourself. Meditation can be a powerful tool to help you find the courage, confidence, clarity, and self-awareness to connect with your truth and express yourself coherently.

Have you ever had a conversation with someone and thought, "I wish I hadn't said that"? You might immediately feel tightness in your jaw. Or perhaps you're struggling to communicate your needs and boundaries and your throat tightens up. Perhaps you've found yourself in relationships or doing work you don't believe in and you feel disconnected from your inner truth. It's a discomforting feeling when your head and heart are in battle with one another and sometimes you may feel that viscerally. By learning to spend a few moments meditating you will be able to quiet your mind and tap into your inner wisdom. From that place, you will be able to make decisions about how to move forward in the most genuine loving way.

This meditation is about finding a little more freedom in the muscles around and within your larynx, which is where your vocal chords are located. It will help you release any unwanted negativity, worry, or stress from the jaw and face. As a professional actor, singer, and teacher this meditation has been paramount in my practice but has also helped me connect to my personal truth. I hope it brings you the freedom it brings to me.

We will connect with our fifth energy center and the color blue to open up the voice box with grace and ease.

INTENTION
I envision blue like an ocean wave of energy, flowing and soothing through my throat.

MEDITATION (FOR AUDIO VERSION SEE PAGE 141)

1. Be seated in a comfortable position. Before we begin the meditation, take your hands into a light fist and bring the knuckles of the fingers to your face, into the space where your upper and lower jaw meet. Feel the muscles with the knuckles and lightly massage in circles, around in one direction and then around in the opposite direction. This may be a little painful so a light touch is recommended or whatever pressure feels good to you. Do this until you feel the jaw release a little.

2. Now rest your hands lightly on your lap. Take a full deep breath in through the nose, hold it, and then exhale out a big audible sigh. Repeat, taking two more breaths.

3. Next take three Lion's Breaths (see page 32). Inhale deeply, and as you exhale stick the tongue right out of the mouth and roar like a lion. Repeat twice more.

Now relax, relax, relax your entire body.

4. The shoulders slide down the back and the vertebrae of the spine ascend upward, each one stacked on top of the other. Bring your attention to your skull; feel the skull resting easy on top of the neck. Relax the muscles of the face. Soften the frown of the forehead. Relax the eyebrows and eyelids, with the eyeballs heavy in the sockets of the skull. Relax your nose, nostrils, and both your cheeks. Relax your ears. Relax the jaw so there is space between the upper and lower teeth in the mouth. Relax your tongue and gums.

5. Bring your attention directly to your throat. Allow yourself to swallow perhaps a couple of times so the attention is right there.

6. Notice for any tightness, pain, or any holding on at the throat. Keep focusing and send all your breath right into that space. Take deep breaths in and out.

7. This is our fifth energy center and it governs our ability to speak our own truth. The color is blue like an ocean, a swirling wave of energy flowing, soothing, and glowing through the throat. Imagine this blue color like a wheel of light at the throat.

8. Spend a little time breathing and notice any emotions that come up here at the throat. There is no need to attach to the emotions, just watch them coming and going like waves. If there is one particular emotion that comes up here, feel free to name it out loud. It could be guilt, blame, sadness, anger... whatever you are feeling, say and declare it to release it. If you can't label the emotion, then declare to release the sensation, for example "tightness."

" I release...........
"I release...........
"I release...........

9. Remember you are not your thoughts. If your thoughts were like the clouds, then you are the sky. Always be the observer. Allow yourself a moment to step back and watch and feel.

Be receptive—Namaste.

How to advance this practice

If you feel some release at the throat, then move your attention to the tongue and focus on releasing and relaxing the tongue. You might find the muscle of your tongue feels busy to begin with, but with time, you will feel it softening in the space of your mouth. You can do this practice anywhere around the body where your emotions are feeling trapped.

Om Improvement: *Mantra for freedom*

You may initially want to skip past this meditation because it involves using your voice and chanting! But stick with it—even if you think you can't sing, it doesn't matter. This is all about the vibration. I absolutely love this meditation. The resonant sound of "Om" gives me a release in the throat and connects me to my lower energy centers. I definitely think you should give it a go!

Om Mantra Japa

Om Mantra Japa is the repetition of the word Om or Aum. If you're not used to chanting Om you may feel silly when you first practice it, but just follow the instructions and observe what happens. OM or AUM is the sacred sound of the universe. Everything has energy and all energy is a wave, therefore all energy is frequency and vibration; that vibration is Om. The ancient yogis believed this sound contains everything: the sound of the wind, the rain, the opening of a flower, your heartbeat; this sound is the life force that runs through your veins. The sound Om is pure, stable, and extremely grounding.

The word "mantra" means a tool for the mind. We use the Om to help our minds deeply focus. Japa is the process of meditative repetition. Practising Om Mantra Japa helps to open energy channels within the body and connects us to our divine spiritual energy. I highly recommend that you experience practicing Om with other people. When groups of people are chanting Om together in harmony it's as if you can feel the earth move!

When you chant Om, let it be as deep and resonant as possible. The Om starts with an open mouth for the Ohhhh and then a closed mouth about halfway through to complete the "mmmmnnn." As you close the mouth you should feel the resonant vibration. Practice alone or join me on the audio—as always, use headphones so you can be fully immersed.

INTENTION
I welcome the power of Om.

A note for practicing Ujjayi (victorious) breath
In this meditation you will practice Ujjayi breath. Take an inhale, imagining you are sucking the air in through a straw at the throat. As you exhale out through the mouth, make the sound "haaaaaaaaa." Practice this for a few breaths, and then try exhaling with the mouth closed while continuing to make the "haaaa" sound. You will inhale and exhale through the nose but feel the breath at the throat—this is Ujjayi.

MEDITATION (FOR AUDIO VERSION SEE PAGE 141)

1. Sitting comfortably, rest your hands on your knees or in your lap and begin to connect with your natural breath.

2. As the breath begins to slow down, lengthen, and deepen, see if you can find your Ujjayi (victorious) breath. This is a loud breath practice that is deep and nourishing and can be heard at the throat; it sounds like an ocean wave. Spend a little time to feel steady and empowered by victorious breath.

Now begin Om Mantra Japa.

3. Take a deep breath in and as you breathe out you'll sing or chant a deep long Ommmmmmmmmmm, right the way through your exhalation. When complete, take a nice easy inhale and repeat Ommmmmmmmmmm.

4. Practice 21 Oms in total. If you're feeling adventurous and you have the time you could continue to 108 Oms. The number 108 represents unity, wholeness, and oneness within the universe.

5. When you have finished Om Mantra Japa, simply observe its powerful effects in silence.

Be receptive—Namaste.

Step into Your Future: *Express yourself through movement*

Time for something else a little bit different! I do hope you give this one a try even if at first it might feel a little "out of the comfort zone" for some.

Moving meditation is a practice that involves combining mindfulness and concentration with physical movement. We've already practiced walking meditation (see page 70), but now we will allow our bodies the freedom of full movement. Engaging in a moving meditation can be a powerful way to release your body's tightness and pent-up emotions, to reduce stress, and to improve your overall wellbeing. It will encourage you to be present in the moment, tune in to any bodily sensations, and express yourself completely freely through your movement. You'll also feel a boost in your circulation and a wonderful rush of endorphins (happy hormones) as a result!

Move and let the energy flow...

Movement can be a powerful form of expression, which allows us to connect deeply with ourselves and communicate with others without the need for any words at all. I always say that movement was my first introduction to meditation at just three years old when I started going to dance class. Of course, I didn't know I was meditating but the feeling I would get dancing in class or performing in shows and competitions, filled my body with a powerful

energy that is difficult to describe. When I danced I felt a cocktail of feelings such as freedom, lightness, connection, joy, and love. I was so incredibly lucky to get paid to dance and make it my career for many years. Unsurprisingly, as an adult I was also drawn to the physical practice of Yoga Asana, which is a mind and body moving meditation. A match made in heaven for me!

From dance to sport to acrobatics, movement can help us convey our emotions, tell stories, and bring forth new ideas. Movement feels primal and is also an integral part of tradition, celebration, and rituals in many cultures.

By incorporating movement into your mindfulness practice like we will do next, you can tap into your body's natural rhythms and experience a deeper sense of connection with yourself. Moving meditation can be a transformative tool for self-expression and personal growth. So kick off your shoes and get ready to freely abandon yourself to the rhythms of either the accompanying audio track, or find a piece of music for yourself, turn the volume right up, and enJOY.

INTENTION

This is my journey from movement to stillness.

MEDITATION (FOR AUDIO VERSION SEE PAGE 141)

1. Start by standing in the middle of your room away from any precious objects or art, so that you can feel the freedom of your movement without any worry. If standing isn't comfortable for you, you can do this in the comfort of a chair.

2. Close your eyes or keep them open with a steady soft gaze. Start here with your hands in a prayer or flat on your heart center and set the following intention. Your intention is to move in a way that feels good, right, and safe for you, discovering exactly how your body needs to move today.

3. Before we begin, take a moment just to shake the body. You could shake your right leg, then your left leg, shake your right arm and left arm, give your head a gentle shake to free up your neck and shoulders, and then shake your entire body. Feel the energy beginning to awaken!

4. You could wind out your wrists and ankles in circles, you could take your arms above your head and reach up for the sky, you could drop your arms down to the floor and fold over your legs. Move your body in any way at all that feels good.

5. Now, since no one is watching, begin to move with abandonment. No choreography, your own made up dance. Perhaps you start off with a gentle sway from side to side, perhaps you gently spin, then explore all the levels, reaching up high and getting down low. Continue swirling and whirling and allowing tightness in the body to release. Move to the beat or rhythm of the sound, and feel the music's vibration into every cell of your being, releasing any energy blockages. You are free to express yourself through your movement.

6. Continue for about 5–10 minutes or for as long as you wish. This is your journey from movement back to stillness. When you've finished, lay yourself down, either on the floor, your sofa, or a bed and feel and observe your elevated heart rate. Feel the energy pulsing through your veins and the wonderful buzz of endorphins.

Give thanks to yourself for this time to let go and surrender to the power of your movement—Namaste.

Chapter Six

Creation

Do you believe you create your own reality?

Welcome to four meditations on creation and creating the life you want to live—this is where things really start to get interesting! Some people think that life just happens to them, but they forget that every day they are constantly making decisions and having interactions and experiences that shape and mold every experience in their lives. You have a great power to create your life exactly the way you want it, but you must focus your thoughts and beliefs and then take the required action when you're ready to move in the direction of your goals.

It all starts with your brain. You experience something in your environment (a person, a place, or a thing); you see, hear, smell, taste, and/or touch it. Your brain triggers a response and produces a thought and an emotion or a feeling. This feeling then influences how you perceive the world around you and how you act.

Stimulus > Thought (brain) > Feeling (body) > Act (response)

The thoughts that you repeat over and over again become your beliefs, which then continue to affect how you think, feel, and act—
the cycle continues.

Like attracts like.

The way you show up in life really does influence what comes back to you. Have you noticed that when you're in a great mood, you tend to meet with other people who have a smile on their face and who are feeling the same. However, when you're in a bad mood, you're likely to encounter a rude storekeeper or a driver with road rage. This is because like attracts like and everything is energy. To put it another way, everything is a wave, a frequency, or a vibration.

By focusing on positive thoughts and beliefs, you can attract positive experiences and shape your reality to align with your goals and desires. Just as you would tune your radio to the frequency of the station you'd like to listen to, you have to tune the frequency of your energy to align with what you desire in order to receive it—this is the Law of Attraction (see The Teachings of Abraham books on page 138). That is not to say there are not ups and downs—these are part of the human experience. But you can create more of the ups if that is where your focus is predominantly.

The following meditations are all about raising your vibrational energy so that you can begin to bring it into alignment with the energy of your dreams. Let's create!

Meditations in this chapter

Igniting Creativity: *Finding the vision*

In today's fast-paced, busy world, it can be challenging to find the time and space to allow our minds to be quiet enough to explore and create freely. Igniting our creativity requires a clear mind, an openness to new ideas, but also plenty of energy and life force. By carving out the time to meditate and by trying out different breathing techniques like the one we will practice in this meditation, we can tap into our inner creativity and our prana—that vital life force that lies deep within our spine.

Unlock new perspectives and feel more alive and energized!

The yogis believe that our creative energy is drawn from a well in our bodies at the base of our spine. This is the location of the first energy center and it is where this prana energy originates from. We focused on the first energy center in the first meditation, Arriving: Meditation for new beginnings (see page 32).

4–16–8 breath technique

Once the lungs are empty you'll inhale for 4 counts, hold for 16 counts, and exhale for 8 counts. Try this with me now. Exhale and empty your lungs as much as you can. Then when you're ready take a very large, long, slow, and deep breath in and pull the breath right up the spine for 4 slow counts. Hold the breath into the brain for 16 counts, and then take a long exhalation for 8 counts to release the breath.

Its energy is so powerful, grounding us deeply into the present. It also surrounds our reproductive organs, containing all the energy to be able to create new life.

In order to feel more energized our brain needs some of this energy. In fact, we use this energy to help unlock all the other energy centers. We've focused on five energy centers so far, and our brain is believed to house our sixth center.

We start this meditation with an invigorating breath practice, followed by a short visualization into your sixth energy center. I personally love this breath—you will literally feel your brain tingling with energy! If you have high blood pressure or are pregnant, do not hold the breath. Just breathe deeply and visualize the rising path of your breath right up your spine.

INTENTION
I ignite my creative spark.

**SIXTH ENERGY CENTER/INDIGO OR PURPLE
WHEEL OF LIGHT ENERGY**
Associations: Intuition, mysticism, creativity

MEDITATION (FOR AUDIO VERSION SEE PAGE 141)

1. Sit up with the spine nice and straight and the shoulders fully relaxed, preparing yourself for this energizing 4–16–8 breath.

2. Before we start, become aware of your natural breath: its depth, its speed, its rhythm. Observe how it is today. No need to apply stories about why it is the way it is, just watch it and soften any tension around it. Notice its sensation within you. Spend a minute or so here.

3. Continue to breathe in this soothing way and bring your attention down to the lowest part of the spine. This is where

the journey of your breath will start. In preparation, just visualize the path it will take in a moment: as you strongly and powerfully inhale, the breath will go upward, along the same path taken by your cerebral spinal fluid, right up, following the line of your spine and into your brain. Next there will be a hold. At this point you will feel the pelvic floor squeeze, pull your navel back into your spine, and tilt your chin slightly to your chest, so that the tongue rests into the upper palate of your mouth just behind the ridge of the teeth. Here we will hold

for about 16 counts or whatever you are comfortable with, and then exhale and let the breath fall down the front of the body.

4. Okay, let's go! When you are ready, take a long, full, deep exhalation, allowing your lungs to empty completely. Then at the bottom of the breath, take a long, slow, deep inhalation through the nose right the way in, for 4 slow counts. On this inhale, feel the breath energy move through your lower back, middle back, between your shoulder blades, upper back, between your shoulders, and up the back of your neck right up to the brain.

5. Now hold the breath for 16 counts. See the breath energy like a light (purple, blue, or white) and play with the energy. Let it spin in the brain, let it dance, make a figure eight. Keep holding until you reach 16.

6. Then exhale slowly through the nose or mouth for 8 counts, feeling the energy fall like water down the front of your body.

7. Return to natural breath, then when you're ready, go for a second round (steps 4–6).

8. Once you get the hang of this breath try it with your eyes closed.

9. You can repeat this breath just a few times or build up to 8 rounds.

10. Once you've completed your final round, take a moment to relax, contemplate, and feel the power of your purple sixth energy center and the tingly sensation of energy in your brain.

Be receptive—Namaste.

This meditation is a fantastic warm up for any of the other meditations in this book, or you can use it on its own in the morning, afternoon, or anytime you need an energy boost.

Your Genius Brain: *Meditation for mental clarity*

In this meditation we focus on the most interesting and certainly the most complex part of the human body—the brain!

Our brain has the ability to change, adapt, remember, learn new things, and increase its capacity even into old age, if given our care, respect, and attention. The brain is an organ not a muscle, but just as you might train a muscle in the gym to make it stronger, with the discovery of neuroplasticity, science has found that you can also train your brain and make it stronger too. Neuroplasticity, also known as neural plasticity or brain plasticity, refers to your brain's ability to change and adapt throughout the course of your life. It is the brain's ability to reorganize itself by forming new neural connections or strengthening existing ones in response to experience, injury, disease, or changes in the environment. Neuroplasticity is essential for learning, creating new habits, and memory, and it plays a critical role in recovery from brain injury or stroke.

Welcome to this meditation for mental clarity. It is one of my favorite meditations in this book, and I recommend you practice it often. You could do it every day for a week or so, and then once you are feeling some changes, perhaps keep it in your routine at least once a week going forward. It's a great check-in to how your brain is operating and responding. During the meditation I will guide you to bring focus to each hemisphere of your brain: the left side, which is mostly responsible for logic and reasoning, and the right side, which is mostly responsible for creativity and speech. By doing this, you will explore how your brain is feeling and remind it of its potential for creativity, problem-solving, and innovation.

There are many other fun ways to train your brain, for example through sudoku, crosswords, jigsaw puzzles, playing chess, or starting a new hobby—anything that requires you to use your cognitive functions. Looking after your brain in this way may help to:

- Reduce stress in the mind and therefore the body

- Improve your mood and enhance your positivity

- Improve your communications

- Help with memory

- Increase your focus, attention, and concentration

- Improve creativity and mental flexibility

- Increase your mental capacity and agility

INTENTION
I quiet my mind and tune into the power of my genius brain!

MEDITATION
(FOR AUDIO VERSION SEE PAGE 141)

1. Prepare for your meditation by coming into a seated position with your hands resting on your knees or thighs, and with your palms facing up toward the sky.

2. Lift your face a little, so that the chin is parallel to the floor. This will mean that the forehead turns slightly up, so that when you close your eyes you can feel a mild focus between your eyebrows. Now relax your shoulders and relax your face, forehead, cheeks, and jaw.

3. Stay focused, with your attention between the eyebrows (or third eye). Breathe exclusively through the nose and imagine the breath moves in and out through that third eye space.

4. Continue breathing, every single breath a fresh supply of oxygen to the brain, washing and cleansing the mind. Keep breathing exclusively through the nose.

5. Find a rhythm that feels soothing and easy to you now, the breath polishing away the dust of agendas, conversation, and of critical thought.

6. If the traffic of your mind is busy and heavy, just gently remind yourself to come back to your breath.

7. Visualize the brain within the chamber of the skull. See its left hemisphere, see its right hemisphere. Observe any differences or similarities in how the sides feel. It's okay if you can't feel anything yet, just trust the process.

8. Bring your attention to the left side of the brain. Breathe into the left side. Remember how it feels when you are clear-minded, when your life is in order. What does it feel like to have a good conversation with someone, when something feels logical, when your brain is working analytically, or when you are sure about things in your life? As you continue to breathe here, feel completely awake within this left side. Feel expansive, open, and clear... feel awake but with a sense of harmony and peace.

How does it feel to begin to soothe that area of the brain?

Enjoy this feeling!

9. Bring the attention now to the right side of the brain; it may take you a few moments to shift your focus. Breathe into the right side. Remember how it feels when you are relaxed and your imagination is free to daydream, when your intuition is strong and you are clear-minded and easily able to express your emotions and your creativity. As you continue to breathe here, feel completely awake within this right side. Feel expansive, open and clear... feel awake but with a sense of harmony and peace.

Enjoy this feeling!

10. We continue now by switching attention from left to right—training the brain to strength, harmony, and clarity.

   Feel the left side of the brain.
   Feel the right side of the brain.
   Left side.
   Right side.
   Left side—awake.
   Right side—awake.
   Left side—harmony, peace.
   Right side—harmony, peace.
   Left side—expansive, open, clear.
   Right side—expansive, open, clear.
   Harmonize one to the other.

11. Now drop your chin gently down toward your chest, keeping the eyes closed. Bring the attention from your brain down into your heart. And breathe into the heart. If it helps, bring your hands to a prayer at the heart center or just place your palms flat on your heart.

   Breathe into the heart—
   feel awake in the heart.

   Breathe into the heart—
   feel harmony within the heart.

   Breathe into the heart—
   feel expansive, open, and clear.

12. Your brain and heart are both awake but with a deep sense of peace. Observe how that feels.

Same feeling—brain to heart. Same feeling— heart to brain.

When you feel the time is right slowly, very slowly, open your eyes.

Be receptive—Namaste.

After this meditation, contemplate how it felt. Where did you feel tightness or difficulty, and where did you find freedom? Perhaps take a moment to journal about your experience or share it with a friend.

Manifesting: *Getting clear on your goals*

What do you really want? If you could be anything, do anything, or have anything in the entire world—go big... what would it be? Grab a piece of paper and write it down so you can see it. It could be a new relationship, a new job, better communication with your family, to have more money, or to enjoy a specific experience. It might be wanting something for others, world peace, or more food and resources for underprivileged children. This is your moment to choose anything!

Now think about how it would make you feel if your dream came true and you got that one thing. What emotions would you feel? Also write those down. For example, "It would make me feel... happy, joyful, relaxed, excited, relieved, expansive, loving, unlimited"—write down any emotion that comes to mind.

We all have things we want in life, and we are allowed to want them... but sometimes we don't give ourselves the permission to allow them into our lives. This meditation is all about daydreaming and most importantly how it would feel to have what you want.

When you were at school you were probably told off for daydreaming. It was considered zoning or spacing out. I was always daydreaming. I loved it and I couldn't stop— it was a calm resting place for my brain. Now I understand and appreciate the power of my daydreams, as they have helped me achieve many of my goals through focus and feeling.

In this meditation you're going to take your mind on a daydreaming vacation by imagining future versions of yourself. Let your mind abandon your everyday reality and begin to create the life and the future you really desire, by aligning your energy and the vibrational frequency (see page 126) of your feelings. Remember all energy is wave and all energy moves at a specific frequency. When we are feeling undesirable emotions (such as depression, guilt, blame, or unworthiness) our energy frequency is low, and we feel tired and de-energized. With upbeat, desired emotions such as joy, love, or excitement, our energy frequency is high and we have more energy.

Find the energy of your future—notice how it feels, find its frequency, and become that reality.

In the beginning of this book we practiced being present and mindful in the NOW, but now we are at "Creation," I want you to allow your mind to expand and wander into glorious thoughts of your future. Bask and bathe in your dreams and allow them to uplift your energy to your greater power.

INTENTION
I am living the life I desire.

MEDITATION (FOR AUDIO VERSION SEE PAGE 141)

1. Get in a comfortable position with your eyes gently closed and let all the awareness tune directly into your breath. Come to your natural exhale and then...

2. Take a full breath in, feeling the whole of the lungs inflate. Exhale and let it go through the nose or mouth. Repeat twice more.

Relax, relax, relax...

3. Bring to mind what it is you want in your future. Think about the feelings and emotions you would have if you got exactly what you want... perhaps relief, freedom, joy, excitement, love, expansion, peace, calm, happiness... anything that comes to mind. What do those emotions feel like within your body? Spend a few minutes here.

4. Imagine now that a figure of a person has emerged in front of you, standing a short distance away from where you now sit in meditation. This person looks like you and it is you living your future reality. This reality may be next week, next month, or next year. This person has already achieved what you desire. Notice the way the future you stands, the way they might walk and talk, the energy in their bones, muscles, and cells. Feel the essence of their presence, and see the smile on their face and the soft peaceful look in their eyes.

5. Now imagine you are within that figure, right inside, and you are that person. See through that person's eyes. Feel the energy and the emotions of your future manifested. Imagine yourself standing and looking back with the same smile and soft peaceful gaze upon the old you who is sitting there in meditation right now. Be proud of that person for taking the time to invest in their future. Feel deep gratitude for your meditation practice and the time you spend to work on yourself. Notice that feeling of gratitude and appreciation within your body.

6. As you stand here, be aware there is another figure standing a little further away. This figure is also YOU looking at both versions of you. This is 80, 90, 100-year-old you looking back on YOU from your future. This person has an even bigger smile on their face—they are so proud and happy that you lived the life you wanted and created for yourself. Now become this person and feel their feelings. Spend some time here.

What does your 80-year-old self want you to do and want you to know?

7. Remember that if you're unhappy or dissatisfied with your life, you have the power to change it. It all starts with your thoughts. As you bring your attention back to your new reality right NOW, notice that wonderful energizing air around you. The sensation of this energy invigorates you. When the time is just right, you can open your eyes.

*Deep, deep gratitude—
Namaste.*

Wishes Fulfilled: *Infinite possibilities*

There are literally infinite paths in your life that you could take, but which path would you like to travel along? Wishes Fulfilled is a powerful practice that works on the "Law of Assumption" which I was first introduced to by the great spiritual teacher Neville Goddard (see page 138). I can tell you it works.

In this meditation, which is my version of Neville Goddard's approach, you will use the Law of Assumption to assume that your wish, dream, or manifestation has already happened. You do this by ignoring the present state of your reality and what is in front of you, and you continue to believe that your wish has been fulfilled until it actually has! How does it work? Well, eventually your energy rises to match the frequency of the vibration of what it is you want, and it cannot not happen (see page 126). You are sort of tricking your mind and your energy into a state of expansion, growth, and abundance. Now you may think this one is completely bonkers. Other people might think you are a bit crazy! So...

Keep this a personal, private quest to achieving your dreams.

Keep focusing relentlessly on whatever it is you want as if it has already manifested in your life, and act and feel just like you would if you already had it. This takes our meditation one step further in that it is something you can practice all the time, on and off your "meditation seat" so to speak—you should stay completely determined and unwavering about it.

I used this technique to manifest my career as an actor and dancer in the West End, my beautiful dog Hicks (named after Abraham Hicks who co-wrote the book *The Law of Attraction*!), the relationship I wanted, the car I wanted, the house with the garden I wanted... and I continue to use it to build up my desires into my future! It seems like sorcery or magic, but I think it's a simple technique of raising energy in line with what you really want—give it a try.

INTENTION
I am living the life of my dreams—I feel it!

MEDITATION
(FOR AUDIO VERSION SEE PAGE 141)

1. You can be lying down or seated. Bring your awareness directly to your breath. Feel it flowing in and feel it flowing out.

2. Watch and release any thoughts as they arrive. Rather than attaching to any one thing, simply notice the thoughts come and go. Continue this step until you feel the traffic of your mind becoming calm and peaceful, for however long this takes you.

3. Now picture a scene from your future, as if the scene has arrived on a TV screen in front of you. See yourself in that vision, see your face, and see your smile. Notice your body language. Who are you with? Stay focused.

4. Begin to time travel! You gently float up from your body and slowly and calmly travel deep into space, traveling past our moon, sun, planets, and stars, into the infinity of beyond. Enjoy this time-traveling experience, letting your imagination guide you as you fly. You see a vision of planet Earth beneath you and as you float back down toward it, you arrive in the life of your dreams. You are no longer watching the screen, you are now inside the screen and you are now that person. See through the eyes of your future you. For that is now the present you. Notice the colors around you. Bring your senses alive. Who are you with? Feel your power and feel your emotions.

How does it feel to be you? How does it feel to have everything you desire?

5. As you bring yourself out of the meditation, allow yourself to bask in the feeling. Don't pay so much attention to what is or isn't around you. Now you begin to live in the energetic vibration of your future self. Now you are the creator!

Be receptive to the power of the highest self—Namaste

Chapter Seven

Appreciation

Everything can come from within.

Both being in a state of appreciation AND feeling that you are appreciated have a powerful effect on your mind, body, and soul. When you are deeply appreciating, you are expressing a state of deep gratitude for something that has now, or has in the past, had a significant effect on your life.

When you appreciate, you connect with your heart and as a result you may feel a sense of peace and clarity within your mind and a "warm glow" or feeling of joy within your body. Appreciation is often calm, steady, and sure. You are honoring not only that person, place, or thing, but also the value and magnitude of it within your life.

Being appreciated by someone else can also feel quite wonderful. Feeling appreciated helps us to establish deep connections, build our confidence, and offers us the space and feeling of safety that allows free expression and creativity in the moment. Although being appreciated is a great "excuse" to feel good, it isn't necessary that you be appreciated in order to feel Present, Balanced, Confident, Connected, Expressive, and Creative. As you've been learning through this book, everything can come from within. You don't need to rely on anyone else for your happiness... If you are appreciative, you will just be happy anyway!

*Appreciation is like sending out
a stream of good vibes.*

Isn't it nice to know and understand the empowering effects that your appreciation has not only on yourself but also on other people? The act of appreciation increases not only our own sense of self-worth, gratitude, and happiness, but also adds to the health and wellbeing of others too. If I could teach everyone in the whole world one thing, it would be how to connect to your heart using the art of appreciation. That way we all would have a more positive outlook on life, which would create more supportive and caring communities.

The following meditations are going to tap into your energy and power so that it becomes easy to feel appreciative as you move through your life. Why do we practice this? Well... why else? Simply because it feels sooooo good!

Meditations in this chapter

A New Path: *Gratitude for all things*

Gratitude helps us to focus on the positive aspects in our life. When we focus our mind, attention, and energy on the process of gratitude, we begin to make new and healthier neurological connections and rewire our brain so that we are less stressed and more optimistic.

This meditation starts with a breathing exercise to get deeper into the positive "zone." I like to call this "Positive Breathing." It helps to clear the sinuses and brings a fresh supply of oxygen to the brain. We will use the Vishnu Mudra hand gesture that we used in Fight, Flight to Freedom (see page 49).

Positive breathing and this gratitude meditation can be practiced in the morning or evening: in the morning to energize, wake up the brain, and inspire your day, and in the evening to bring you clarity and prepare your brain and body for a calm, deep sleep.

Try out this little gratitude exercise

Take a pen and paper and think of at least 50 people, places, or things in your life that you are deeply grateful and appreciative for, and write them down. This should be a simple task. You may get on a roll and think of 100–200 things.

These things can be as simple as…"I'm grateful for my morning cup of coffee, my child's beautiful smile, birdsong…," right through to any bigger things you've created in your life. You may be grateful to people from your past for the lessons they taught you (good and bad) which caused your life to expand. It doesn't matter however seemingly big or small they are, write them all down so you can clearly see them.

Now once you've done that, observe… How did it make you feel?

Re-read your list and add to it whenever you feel inspired.

INTENTION

I step onto a new path of deep gratitude.

MEDITATION

(FOR AUDIO VERSION SEE PAGE 141)

1. Start this meditation in a seated position. Let your awareness drift inward and check in: how are you feeling today? Allow the breath to slow down, deepen, and expand until you feel at peace and at one with the breath.

2. Allow every breath to release the thoughts, conversations, tasks, and agendas of the day. There is nothing to do but breathe, and enjoy the life force, energy, and freedom you find within your breath. (Spend a couple of minutes here.)

Start with positive breathing.

3. Bring your right hand into Vishnu Mudra (see page 49). First of all take a breath in through both of the nostrils and a breath out through both nostrils, then use the right thumb to gently seal the right nostril, leaving the left nostril open...

4. Take 8 long slow, deep breaths exclusively through the open side. Try inhaling for 5 seconds and exhaling for 5 seconds. No rush. Take your time. The whole of

your awareness is on the breath. Feel its sensation. Feel its temperature—cool as you breathe in and warm as you breathe out. Keep your eyes closed if you can. Stay focused.

5. After the final exhale of those 8 breaths, rest your right hand down and now breathe through both nostrils deeply, for about 3 steady rounds. Feel the effect of positive breathing and the difference between the right and left nostrils.

6. Let's move to the other side. We will use the same hand (the right hand) and the same Vishnu Mudra. Take a breath in through both nostrils and breathe out. Now take your arm across the body and use your ring finger (the one next to your pinkie) to seal off the left nostril, leaving the right nostril open. Repeat steps 4–5... Then move to step 7.

Notice how easy it is to breathe.

7. Feel the air right through your nostrils and your sinuses, down the back of your throat and deep into your lungs. Fresh nourishing oxygen, energy, life force—feel it and enjoy it... Notice how refreshed the mind feels—focused and calmly energized.

8. Let your mind drift now to all those things you are deeply grateful for in your life. Visualize them as images, as through you are watching them on a screen in your mind, with vibrant colors and sounds. Notice the sensations of peace, happiness, joy, and satisfaction they bring you. Perhaps they even make you smile! Bask in this moment.

9. Finally, visualize a path out in front of you. This could be a long, straight path, or a winding country path awash with a beautiful sunrise or sunset. Design your path in your mind however you want it to look. You are walking, running, or dancing along this path. You see things you're grateful for when you interact with them and you keep moving forward, always changing, always evolving, and always expanding.

This is your path to an even greater life. There is always more to experience in life—it just keeps getting better. Walk the new path, be grateful, and enjoy! Namaste.

Attracting Abundance: *Raising your vibrational energy*

We all desire to feel abundant, whether that be from a fulfilling career, financial abundance, strong and loving relationships, or whatever else it is that we dream of for our lives. Meditation can be a powerful tool to help attract what you desire, as it allows you to train your thoughts and emotions to create a more positive and abundant mindset. Once we've trained the mind to become more receptive to ideas of abundance, then your mindset will be more abundant and so too your life.

In the Creation chapter (see page 104) we did a lot of visualization to help us manifest and create. But in this meditation we will use the energy that is all around us, along with the power of our feelings to help increase our energy so that it aligns with the free-flowing, unlimited abundance that the universe has to offer. Our seventh energy center is located about 12 inches (30 centimeters) above the crown of the head, and it helps us to connect to the oneness and wholeness of literally everything; of all of the energy in the entire universe!

INTENTION
I align with free-flowing, unlimited abundance.

MEDITATION (FOR AUDIO VERSION SEE PAGE 141)

1. In whatever position is most comfortable for you and with your eyes closed, imagine you are out in a beautiful expansive field on a warm sunny evening surrounded by nature, wildflowers, and butterflies. It is dusk, you hear the final sounds of birdsong, and you can already see the twinkle of the night stars.

2. You are safe, protected, and deeply connected in nature. You begin to feel a wheel of violet light energy (so bright it is almost white) spinning about 12 inches (30 centimeters) above your head. This energy connects you with the wholeness and oneness of the universe. Feel the crown of your head opening your brain up to the infinite possibilities of the universe. (Spend a minute or so here.)

3. Now bring your awareness to your heart and notice what it feels like to be here.

4. Repeat each affirmation to yourself three times, as if each of them were songs directly from your heart—feel every word of every short sentence.

I feel connected to the oneness of the universe.

I flow with the stream of energy around me.

I feel relaxed and happy.

I feel joyful.

I release any fear.

Everything always works out for me.

Things come to me easily.

I release any doubt.

I am pure love.

I am whole.

I am free.

I feel my vibrational energy rise.

Abundance is all around me.

I am deeply grateful—thank you.

5. Now just spend some time basking in deep gratitude and appreciation for this meditation and your time and focused investment in it.

Be receptive—Namaste.

Prism of Light: *Energy center meditation using imagery and colors*

Energy centers, often referred to as Chakras, are points within the body that run along the spine where the energy frequency has been found to be the most concentrated.

So why is the energy more concentrated at these Chakra points?

I mentioned in Part One, Your Powerful Body (see page 18) about the energy centers. One theory is that the energy centers relate to specific glands (which secrete hormones) within the body.

It is believed that energy centers can become blocked with undesirable emotions and cause our hormones to be out of balance, which leads to health problems and even disease. By focusing on the affected center, releasing any stagnant energy, and allowing that center to open up, we can balance and harmonize these centers. This will help to bring our body into hormonal balance, boost our immune system, and can even up-regulate/upgrade certain genes in the body for health and healing.

If you have followed this book consecutively, by now you will have worked with all seven of the energy centers. You may have even been able to feel them on a visceral level. If you haven't followed the book consecutively or still haven't felt the energy centers within your body, then don't worry, you can still dive into

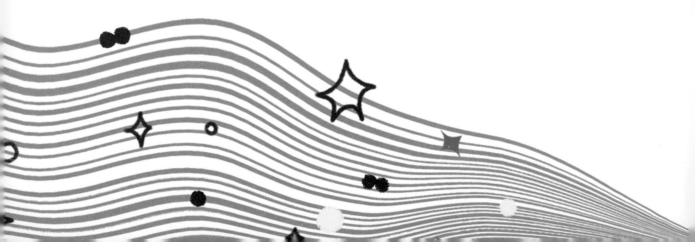

THE ENERGY CENTERS

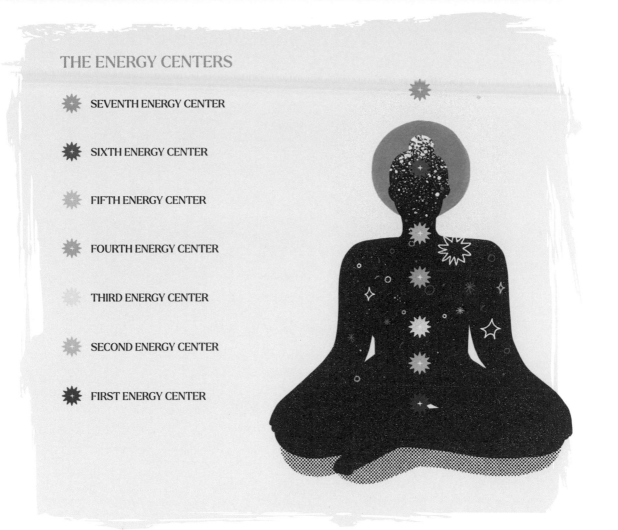

- SEVENTH ENERGY CENTER
- SIXTH ENERGY CENTER
- FIFTH ENERGY CENTER
- FOURTH ENERGY CENTER
- THIRD ENERGY CENTER
- SECOND ENERGY CENTER
- FIRST ENERGY CENTER

and enjoy this meditation and the power it brings you. Exploring the energy centers can offer a transformative and enlightening experience. This meditation is very simple and very visual.

INTENTION
I am PURE ENERGY!

MEDITATION (FOR AUDIO VERSION SEE PAGE 141)

1. Be seated, with your hands resting lightly on your lap, palms open to the sky. Close your eyes and just let the traffic of your mind begin to slow down and become a little quieter.

2. Let your breath flow gently in and out and feel it softly arriving into each and every cell of the physical body. Take a few minutes here as you settle into a rhythm with your breath. Notice how thoughts come and go and fluctuate from one thing to another. Don't force the thoughts out, just be the observer of them.

3. Now guide your focus and attention down your body to the first energy center located just in front of the base of your spine. Imagine a red wheel of light energy spinning at the base of your spine. For this step and for each of steps 4–9: Stay focused on this area for a few minutes.

Feel the energy here, visualize the light. See if you can bring this place into a feeling of harmony and oneness with the universal energy all around you.

4. Bring your attention to the second energy center, located 2 inches (5 centimeters) below the naval and in front of the spine. Imagine an orange wheel of light energy spinning under the navel.

5. Bring your attention to the third energy center located at the solar plexus, the stomach, just under the rib cage. Imagine a yellow wheel of light energy spinning at the solar plexus.

6. Bring your attention to the fourth energy center located at the heart in the center of the chest. Imagine a green wheel of light energy spinning at the heart center.

7. Bring your attention to the fifth energy center located at the throat. Imagine a blue wheel of light energy spinning at the throat.

8. Bring your attention to the sixth energy center located in the middle of the brain, just behind the space between your eyebrows. Imagine a purple wheel of light energy spinning in the brain.

9. Bring your attention to the seventh energy center located at the crown of the head and up to 12–18 inches (30–46 centimeters) above it. Imagine a violet wheel of light energy (so bright it is almost white) spinning just above the crown of the head.

10. Be aware of this beautiful prism of light right up your spine, and follow it with your attention through the red, orange, yellow, green, blue, purple, and bright violet, white light! Feel all the colors glowing out of you, around you, and out in all directions, creating beautiful rainbows and patterns all around your body. Feel gratitude for the energy of colors and for the rainbow of vibrational energy in your entire reality.

Be receptive—Namaste.

Electric Mode: *Ultimate energy meditation*

By now you'll have been able to feel and experience the energy deep within your body and you understand that increasing your energy also increases your power.

I'm sure you're beginning to feel the power of your own energetics, and maybe you have also started to tap into and feel the energy of others. When doing this kind of energy work, it can open us up to a deep sensitivity at first. You may find that you begin to get a bit more picky about which friends you spend time with, how much media and news you watch, and how much negative energy you allow into your life. Once you start to be more aware of your energy, it's like you're an energy connoisseur and you'll just want to protect it. That happens on the path of raising consciousness and spiritual growth; it's completely normal and something to enjoy. Make a commitment to yourself to feel good and protect that at all costs.

Yogis believe that the body has 72,000 very subtle energy channels (Nadis). They are like long pieces of extremely fine hair that run in networks throughout your entire body. They are so incredibly subtle that they cannot even be seen through a microscope, but they are there. These channels are the energy highways of the body and deliver our prana (life force energy) at high speed from one place to another and aid healing. Many other Eastern philosophies also believe in channels or meridians around the body. In Chinese medicine the life force is called Qi (Chi).

We have explored throughout this book many ways to increase our physical and mental energy using the power of the mind, movement, mantra, and also the breath. I've saved this electrical breath practice for the end as a finale as I find it to be incredibly powerful and it's one that often gets requested when I'm teaching a live class. This breath will get your energy high—and that is all I have to say!

INTENTION
I recharge my body, mind, and spirit!

MEDITATION (FOR AUDIO VERSION SEE PAGE 141)

1. Lay down either on your yoga mat or in your bed. You have made the decision to practice this energizing breath today. So set an intention to give it all you've got!

2. Take a moment to scan the body and notice where its energy levels are today, right now, prior to the breath practice.

3. If there is any part of the body that feels tight, stressed, or uncomfortable, bring your attention to it and feel the intensity. Stay with it as long as you need to, until you feel the intensity softening and maybe some release.

4. Let's start. Take a strong inhalation through the nose and a strong sigh out through the mouth. The breath is fairly rapid. Inhale through the nose, exhale and sigh (through the mouth). Inhale nose, exhale mouth, and so on. Try 8 breaths first of all.

5. After 8 breaths, take another inhale, and squeeze and hold everything at the top. Squeeze your hands, feet, face, and eyes closed tight, so that the whole body and every muscle tenses up—hold it—and then relax.

Feel the effect of the breath, like electricity in the body and brain.

6. See if you can build up to 12 breaths on a second round and then maybe you can build up to 20 breaths on a third round. After every round take that inhale, hold, and squeeze before releasing and relaxing and observing the effects of the breath.

7. Now visualize yourself surrounded by a white, blue, and purple light. Feel the electricity in your body. Feel it in your veins. Acknowledge that YOU created that just by using the power of your mind and breath.

8. Relax for as long as you need to after this practice, bathing in an ocean of bright white light. When you're ready to step back into your day, do so with the knowledge that you are now super-powered and in Electric mode!

Nothing can stop you today!
Be receptive—Namaste.

Closing Words: *Integration and Intention Setting*

I hope by now you have started to experience the profound changes and benefits that a meditation practice can have on your physical and mental health, and indeed your overall life. It is my mission to continue to teach meditation as a tool to empower you to empower yourself, by encouraging you to understand and get to know yourself on a deeper level.

So you've finished the book, maybe you've completed all the meditations—what's next?

Well, by integrating meditation into your daily routine, you will continue to experience changes in your life and cultivate a greater sense of inner harmony and balance. These meditations have been designed to be practiced over and over, and all 30 of them could keep you going for many years within your practice. Repetition is key and what I've found through my own practice is that familiarity with meditations is also nourishing. My advice is to continue to dip into this book, choose the one meditation that resonates with you the most in that moment, and practice it every day until you begin to feel shifts. Also see the tips on pages 136–137 to help you. When you feel like you have mastered

that meditation, then choose a different one. We are always changing and so do our preferences and needs. Be aware of this and allow yourself the freedom to go with the flow of life.

By setting intentions and making meditation a priority, you will experience a greater sense of peace and wellbeing in all areas of your life. I wish you all the best with your meditation journey. If you ever have any questions then feel free to contact me via my socials or website.

With deep care,

Clare x

TOP TIPS

Meditate at the same time every day

It takes an average of 66 days to form a habit. For a while you may feel like you're doing it wrong, especially when it feels difficult. Don't give up. Try it for 66 days and see what happens.

Figure out WHY you're practicing

Do you practice meditation to reduce stress and anxiety, to connect more deeply with your spiritual side, to clear and quieten your mind, or purely to feel good? Whatever it is... go with that. Many people have different reasons for practicing. Write down why YOU practice and refer back to it often.

Set an intention often to meditate and to feel your energy rise

An intention is stating your commitment. Be committed to changing your own life.

Try not to get discouraged if you have a "bad meditation"

We all have bad days, and sometimes those bad days and bad meditations can teach us the biggest, most profound lessons.

Take the rough with the smooth

There will be difficult times within your meditation practice as emotions begin to surface. Allow all emotions. Remember there are no bad emotions. Everything is part of the human experience.

Notice when you're falling off track and remember to take care of yourself

Gently remind yourself of your power often, especially when you're going through difficult times. Speak to yourself like you would to your best friend.

Remember your meditation practice is cumulative

Every day you meditate you quieten and explore deeper into your internal space. Every day you are building on the day that came before. There is no end to how good you can feel through a consistent, dedicated practice.

Try quiet meditation

Along with guided meditation, I also integrate quiet meditation into my daily practice. For this I set an alarm on my phone usually for 21 minutes (to give me 1 minute of fidget time!), I simply focus upon my breath and the sounds around me in my environment. If something comes up that I need to think about or work out, I observe and allow that thought to have its moment before I gently remind myself to come back to my breath. If I have negative thoughts, I visualize them as little red negative signs that I gradually turn into larger green positive signs.

Resources and References

66 days to form a habit (see page 136)
https://www.ucl.ac.uk/news/2009/aug/how-long-does-it-take-form-habit

BioMarker explanation (see page 78)
https://www.fiosgenomics.com/examples-of-biomarkers-and-biomarker-data-analysis/

Books that have deeply inspired my life and work

Anatomy Of The Spirit: The Seven Stages Of Power And Healing by Caroline Myss, Ph.D.

Autobiography of a Yogi by Paramahansa Yogananda

Ask and It Is Given: Learning to Manifest Your Desires by Esther and Jerry Hicks (The Teachings of Abraham)

Becoming Supernatural: How Uncommon People Are Doing the Uncommon by Dr. Joe Dispenza

Breaking The Habit Of Being Yourself: How to Lose Your Mind and Create a New One by Dr. Joe Dispenza

Breath: The New Science of a Lost Art by James Nestor

Letting Go: The Pathway of Surrender by David R. Hawkins, M.D., Ph.D.

Living Untethered: Beyond the Human Predicament by Michael A. Singer

Many Lives, Many Masters by Dr. Brian Weiss

The Astonishing Power of Emotions: Your Inner Guide to the Law of Attraction by Esther and Jerry Hicks (The Teachings of Abraham)

The Alchemist by Paulo Coelho (and his many other books)

The HeartMath® Solution by Doc Childre and Howard Martin

The Power of Imagination: The Neville Goddard Treasury by Neville Goddard

The Power of Now: A Guide to Spiritual Enlightenment by Eckhart Tolle

The Source: The Secrets of the Universe, the Science of the Brain by Tara Swart, M.D, Ph.D.

The Road Less Travelled by M. Scott Peck

The Untethered Soul: The Journey Beyond Yourself by Michael A. Singer

The Vortex: Where the Law of Attraction Assembles All Cooperative Relationships by Esther and Jerry Hicks (The Teachings of Abraham)

The Yoga Sutras of Patanjali

Transurfing Reality in 78 Days: A Practical Course in Creating Your Own Reality by Vadim Zealand

When the Body Says No: The Cost of Hidden Stress by Gabor Maté

Yoga Nidra: Swami Satyananda Saraswati

Box breathing used by the Navy Seals (see page 38)
https://www.medicinenet.com/why_do_navy_seals_use_box_breathing/article.htm

DHEA (see pages 17 and 48)
https://www.mountsinai.org/health-library/supplement/dehydroepiandrosterone

Great spiritual teachers of now and recent times

If you want to know more about these people, I strongly recommend you research their ideas and writings for yourself: Abraham Hicks, Alan Watts, Brené Brown, Bruce Lipton, Dr Joe Dispenza, Echart Tolle, Gregg Braden, Michael A. Singer, Mooji, Ram Dass, Sadguru, Thich Nhat Hanh, Wayne Dyer

HeartMath®

HeartMath®'s work has been prevalent within the military, Special Ops, emergency responders, in big business and corporations, in government, with children in schools, and with normal people who just want to navigate everyday stress in this fast-moving world. The HeartMath® tools help people to "improve focus and creativity, elevate emotional clarity, lower stress and anxiety levels, strengthen the immune system, and promote the body's optimal performance."
Quote from the book *The HeartMath® Solution*

"Exploring the Role of the Heart in Human Performance," McCraty, Rollin, *Science of the Heart*, Volume 2, HeartMath Institute, 2015: https://www.heartmath.org/research/science-of-the-heart/

Heart Focused Breathing Technique™ (see page 25) is approved for use courtesy of HeartMath Institute www.heartmath.org

HeartMath® Depletion to Renewal: https://www.heartmath.com/wp-content/uploads/2019/06/Sample-BPRG.pdf

HeartMath® Inner-Ease™ technique (see page 79) is approved for use courtesy of the HeartMath Institute

"Law of Assumption"—Neville Goddard (see page 118)

https://en.wikipedia.org/wiki/Neville_Lancelot_Goddard

"Law of Attraction"—Abraham Hicks (see page 105)

https://www.abraham-hicks.com/ and on YouTube

Mantra meaning—"a tool for the mind" (see pages 27 and 98)

https://www.yogajournal.com/yoga-101/sanskrit/mantras-101-the-science-behind-finding-your-mantra-and-how-to-practice-it/#%23

Namaste

https://www.yogabasics.com/connect/yoga-blog/namaste-meaning/

Neuroscience

If you're interested in delving deeper into understanding the effect of meditation on the brain, I highly recommend neuroscientist Dr. Joe Dispenza's books *Breaking the Habit of Being Yourself* and *Becoming Supernatural*. His pioneering work looks into the effect of meditation on brain wave patterns and the upregulation of proteins, cells, and DNA.

Ujjayi breath (see page 98)

See my video on YouTube:
Clare Connolly Wellness, Ujjayi Pranayama: The Yogic Breath for Balance, Calmness, and Energy, https://www.youtube.com/watch?v=fRfgbwVCwOY&t=377s

QR Codes for Meditation Audio Guides

Here you'll find QR codes which link to the audio versions of the meditations. To use the codes, open the camera on your smart phone or tablet. Point the camera at a QR code, then tap on the link that appears on your screen. Create a free account to listen to the meditation. Alternatively, you can go to www.powerfulyoubook.com and create a free account to listen to the meditation audio guides.

PART ONE: GETTING STARTED

Interoception and Proprioception (see page 20)

Heart Focused Breathing™ from HeartMath® (see page 25)

PART TWO: MEDITATIONS

Chapter One: Presence

Arriving
(see page 32)

Cycle of Life
(see page 34)

Mindful Moment
(see page 38)

Be Here Now
(see page 40)

Chapter Two: Balance

Morning Ritual
(see page 44)

Fight, Flight to Freedom
(see page 48)

Finding Your Equilibrium
(see page 51)

Sleep Ritual
(see page 54)

Chapter Three: Confidence

Locating Your Power
(see page 60)

Your Confident Body
(see page 64)

The Second Brain
(see page 68)

Walking into Confidence
(see page 70)

Chapter Four: Connection

Breathing Heart
(see page 76)

The Inner-Ease™ Technique
from HeartMath® (see page 78)

Expand Your Relationships
(see page 80)

Love Beyond Time
(see page 84)

Chapter Five: Expression

Letting Go
(see page 90)

Finding Your Voice
(see page 94)

Om Improvement
(see page 98)

Step into Your Future
(see page 100)

Chapter Six: Creation

Igniting Creativity
(see page 106)

Your Genius Brain
(see page 110)

Manifesting
(see page 114)

Wishes Fulfilled
(see page 118)

Chapter Seven: Appreciation

A New Path
(see page 122)

Attracting Abundance
(see page 126)

Prism of Light
(see page 128)

Electric Mode
(see page 132)

Index

Acknowledgments

A big heartfelt thank you to so many who have energized me in the writing of this book.

Firstly to my partner Andy who had to put up with me talking non-stop about the "Meditation Book"—thank you for continuously encouraging me particularly through your unwavering dedication to your own meditation practices, and for being a fantastic sounding board and a great support, always unconditional in your love—I am so incredibly lucky and grateful to you.

Also thanks to Mr. Hicks the dog—for his patience with me while I was writing this book, when all he wanted to do was play!

Deep gratitude to my Mum, Dad, sister and my entire family and all my incredible friends for always believing in me, encouraging me, and reminding me that no matter what, I should always follow my path of greatest joy.

Shout out to my dear friend and amazing human Robert Davis, who reminded me to meditate in 2019 when I had lost my way and who encouraged me to record my meditations in audio format way back when.

Thanks to my amazing voice-over Agent Michele Daeche at The Voice Agency for literally EVERYTHING — I could write a book on how grateful I am to you!

Love and thanks to Jo Good (yoga student, turned great friend) and to everyone at BBC Radio London who took "a risk" and put Meditation on to the airwaves in 2020! It worked out well! A special thanks to all the listeners around the world who tuned in and asked us to keep it going to the present day. I love that we can all connect through meditation no matter where or who we are—that's powerful!

A special thanks to commissioning editor Kristine Pidkameny at CICO for being one of those international listeners of the Jo Good show and inviting me to write this book—and then for all the many zoom calls where she helped me extract the contents of the book out of my brain! I'm so grateful for your guidance and contributions.

Also to all the other amazing people at CICO, thank you to Penny Craig and special credit to Jenny Dye for all the kindness, edits, and for answering my many, many questions. Gratitude to Production Manager Gordana Simakovic. I'd also like to acknowledge and praise illustrator Gina Rosas Moncada for the beautifully creative illustrations, combined with the vision of Art Director Sally Powell and Designer Emily Breen—you are all so brilliant—it has been such fun and a privilege to work with all of you at CICO.

A big dose of gratitude to Jonny Martin (JMartMusic) who composed many of the mesmerizing tracks in the audio versions of the meditations—YOU are a huge talent!

Thanks to Alice Hart-Davis (fellow author friend) for your enthusiasm when I confided in you and only you about this project right at the beginning—I needed that pep talk!

Thanks to Ross Grant, Stuart Piper, Matt Wycliffe, Elliot Harper, and Toby Lawrence, my life-long friends, for their spiritual chat, entrepreneurism, technical help, cheerleading, and all round inspiration!

I would also like to recognize all the wonderful folk at the SoundHouse Recording Studios, especially Director Perrin Sledge, Office Manger extraordinaire Freddy Sledge, but also Phil, Mark, Gerry, Wilfredo, Rohan, Rosalind, and Dan (who's always with us in spirit) for the many fun years of working together, but also for helping me with the audio version of this book.

A big shout-out to my HeartMath® family in the USA: Doc Childre, Sheva Carr, Robert Browning, Lisa Gorman, Claire Shafe, Gaby Bohemer, and my fellow HMCT trainees—a big heart hug to you all!

Thank you to all the teachers and light-workers out there who guided me and continue to help me navigate my own path of spiritual growth. Especially to my teacher and guru Sri Dharma Mittra who first taught me how to teach back in 2009—you instilled a great passion in me.

And finally and definitely most importantly THANK YOU to every student I have ever taught whether live or online. YOU are my biggest teachers. Without you and your dedication I wouldn't have had a class to teach, I wouldn't have run the retreats, and I wouldn't have written this book. The community and sense of connection you create is incredible. You keep the fire in my belly and my heart wide open. For you I am MOST GRATEFUL. Namaste Yogis! Peace, Peace, Peace.